# A
# FIRST READING BOOK

IN THE

## MICMAC LANGUAGE:

COMPRISING

THE MICMAC NUMERALS, AND THE NAMES

OF THE DIFFERENT KINDS OF

## BEASTS, BIRDS, FISHES, TREES, &c.

OF THE

MARITIME PROVINCES OF CANADA

ALSO, SOME OF THE

## INDIAN NAMES OF PLACES,

*And many Familiar Words and Phrases,*

TRANSLATED   LITERALLY   INTO   ENGLISH

———————

**HALIFAX:**
NOVA SCOTIA PRINTING COMPANY,
**1875.**

Published by
Global Language Press
Vancouver, B.C. ,
CANADA.

http://www.language-press.com


Wela'lin to So'sep, Mi'gmaq Language Resources Coordinator for
Listuguj for help deciphering words in the original.

http://www.mikmaqonline.org

ISBN 0-9738924-8-X

Printed in the United States of America

OTHER TITLES FROM GLOBAL LANGUAGE PRESS


New Familiar Abenakis and English Dialogues by Joseph
Laurent, first published in 1884.

# PREFACE.

THE primary object of this little work, is to aid the Indians in learning to read. It is also designed to aid them in learning English. Hence every Indian word is translated. They are not *interlined,* but placed opposite, in a separate column, so as to render everything as distinct as possible.

It is believed, too, that many of the white people will be glad to avail themselves of the facility thus afforded for becoming acquainted in some measure with that truly wonderful language, *native Nova Scotian.* As this language contains no sounds that the English vocal organs are not accustomed to, and as by the arrangement adopted the pronunciation and the meaning of every Indian word inserted in the book, can be learned with very little trouble, it is presumed that an important object will be in this respect gained. The writer is happy to know that many of the Micmac Indians have during the last fifteen years learned to read. A small edition of a "Micmac First Reading Book" did good service ; but it has for some time been exhausted. A determination to learn to read has been aroused among the Indians everywhere. It should be fostered by every legitimate means. Such a book as is here presented to the public cannot but be beneficial in promoting so desirable an object. A summary of the contents is given in the title page. While the white children—aye, and older people too— are learning to *count* in Indian, and also learning what the Indians call the animals, &c., &c., they will be *teaching* as well as *learning;* and thus that mutual good-will and confidence which the writer is happy to know has been originated and fostered between the two races, during the last twenty years, will be increased.

It is scarcely necessary to add, that in naming beasts, birds, fishes, trees, plants, &c., &c., in English, pains have been taken to ascertain and give as correctly as possible, the *popular name,* and that alone. Mistakes will doubtless have occurred, but great pains have been taken to avoid them.

# LESSON I.

## THE ENGLISH ALPHABET.

A a,    B b,    C c,    D d,
E e,    F f,    G g,    H h,
I i,    J j,    K k,    L l,
M m,    N n,    O o,    P p,
Q q,    R r,    S s,    T t,
U u,    V v,    W w, X x,
Y y,    Z z.

---

## THE MICMAC ALPHABET.

A a, â, ā, ă,    B b,    C c,    D d,
E e, ĕ,    G g,    H h,    I i, ĭ,    J j,
K k,    L l,    M m,    N n,    O o, ō, ŏ,
P p,    S s,    T t,    U u, ŭ, W w,
Y y, ei,    oo,    ow,    āoo.

NOTE.—In Micmac there are no *silent* letters, and each letter is invariably sounded *one* way: the consonants *c* and *g* being always *hard; ch* as in *church* : and the rest exactly as in English. The vowels are sounded as in the following scale: viz :

| | |
|---|---|
| a as in *father,* | ŏ as in *not,* |
| ā as in *fate,* | u as in *bugle,* |
| â as the second a in *abaft,* | ŭ as in *tub,* |
| ă as in *fat,* | oo as in *fool, move,* |
| e as in *me,* | ŏŏ as in *good, wood,* |
| ĕ as in *met,* | ei as i in *pine, height,* |
| ĭ as in *pin,* | ow as in *cow,* |
| o as in *note,* | āoo as ow *nearly.** |

When a, ā, or e, is *doubled*—thus : aa, āā, ee—the two letters are to be sounded as one, the sound being *prolonged.* In the same manner the accented vowels, ŏ and oo', express simply a *prolonged o* or *oo.* The usual place for the accent in Micmac words, is on the penult. It is marked when it falls on any other syllable. A prolonged vowel is accented of course.

---

* *The exact sounds of ā and* oo *are combined into a dipthong. They form a single syllable; as in* coon-dāoo, *a stone;* kāoo-che, *I am cold.*

# LESSON 2.

| MICMAC. | ENGLISH. |
|---------|----------|
| an, | you say |
| as, | a clam |
| āk, | he is here |
| at, | he says |
| ăp, | again |
| dā, | my comrade |
| na. | this, there |
| wo. | a pot |
| Pĭ. | sit |
| ma, | not |
| mā, | yet |
| ak, | and |
| aa. | ah, aye |
| āā, | yes |
| ek, | if it were there |
| ech. | let him be there |
| kā! | come on! |
| tŭ. | (*sign* of a question) |

| MICMAC. | ENGLISH. |
|---|---|
| moo, | not |
| noo, | O father |
| oot. | this |
| kat. | an eel |
| sōk, | send him away |
| nen, (neen) | I, me |
| eâ'! | oh dear! |
| ān. | { (a familiar term of address for wife or husband) |
| kel, (keel) | thou, thee |
| tan, | who, when |
| San' | John |
| Sak, | Jim |
| pāl. | stay, wait |
| tĕt. | there |
| nŭt. | this |
| ĕlp. | also |
| wĕn. | who, some one |
| lōk. | very |
| nooch. | my father |
| kooch. | thy father |
| pĭch. | let him sit |
| kwes. | O my son |

| MICMAC | ENGLISH. |
|--------|----------|
| toos, | O daughter |
| kwĭlk, | he looks for it |
| wes, | a beaver house; a hay-cock |
| sŭm, | feed him |
| nĭpk | summer |
| nĕpk | he is dead |
| tas? | how many times? |
| tās, | so many times |
| nan | five, five times |
| nek, | my house |
| kek, | thy house: it is sharp |
| wek, | his house |
| wen, | marrow |
| wĭk, | sweet |
| 'ntoon. | my mouth. |

---

## L E S S O N   3 .

dā, as āk: āā, san āt ās āk: moo ās na, kat na, ak āk na tĕt: moo, sak āk na tĕt, ak san āk na tĕt: noo, sŭm sak ak san : aa, kwes, tĕt pĭch san, ak tĕt pĭch sak, ak kel tĕt pĭ: noo, wĕn āt oot? kel tŭ ān oot ? toos, āā: kooch āt oot: nen na: pāl, kā, sŭm sak, sŭm san : ak sŭm kooch: kān, toos, nŭt na ; (nŭt na, that's it.)

## LESSON 4.

| | |
|---|---|
| Wen tŭ keel? | Who art thou ? |
| Nen San, | I am John |
| Kel Sak, | you are Jim |
| ak ĕlp ncoch. | and also my father. |
| pĭ tĕt, kel, | sit you there |
| kooch | your father |
| pĭch oot tĕt, | let him sit there |
| ech tĕt : | let him be there |
| nĕpk ās tŭ? | is the clam dead ? |
| āā, nĕpk ās. | yes, the clam is dead |
| Wĕn āt nĕpk ās ? | who says the clam is dead ? |
| San ăt, ak | John says so, and |
| Sak āt, ak neen. | Jim says so, and I. |
| Tas āt ? | How many times does he say it ? |
| Tās āt, | So many times he says it |
| sest āt, | three times he says it |
| kel ān nan, | you say so five times |
| Toos, | my daughter |
| San āt, | John says |
| wes āk ; | a beaver house is there. |
| Noo', Sak āt, | My Father, Jim says |
| wen āk, | marrow is there |
| ak măls: | and a flint |
| kel ān, | you say |
| moo wes. | it is not a beaver house, |

| | |
|---|---|
| moo mǎls, | it is not a flint |
| moo wen, | it is not marrow |
| moo ās | it is not a clam |
| moo na. | it is not that |
| Dĕs, | if it should be there |
| dĕch. | let it be there |
| mǎls ek, | if a flint is there |
| ech mals, | let the flint be there |
| aa. | aye: so be it. |

---

## LESSON 5.

| | |
|---|---|
| Dā, | My friend. |
| pǐskwa, | come in. |
| baase, | sit down. |
| oo'se, | warm yourself. |
| cheenǔm, | a man. |
| āhk, | is here. |
| wǐgwǒmk, | at the wigwam. |
| asoon, | some cloth. |
| pawǒtk', | he wants it. |
| Tǔlǐm', | tell him. |
| ĕdĕk tea. | it lies there. |
| Pāl! | Hold on! stay! |
| kechka. | a little. |
| etĕs nadāāl, | I will be there. |
| wegǐpch, | soon. |
| Nedǎp', | Comrade. |
| nĕmool', | I see you. |
| ak, | and. |

| | |
|---|---|
| keel nĕmeen. | you see me. |
| ak ĕlp, | and also. |
| neen nĕmeek | I see (him) |
| ŭkwĭs', | your son. |
| ak nĕmeek | I see (her) |
| ŭktoos', | your girl. |
| Nĕmeek 'ntoos, | I see my daughter. |
| ak noodâk' | and I hear (him). |
| 'nkwĭs. | my son. |
| Nĕmeek | I see her |
| ābĭt, | a woman. |
| Noodâk | I hear him |
| cheenŭm, | a man. |
| Mogwā', | no. |
| sesĭp' noodâk. | a bird I hear. |
| Tame? | where ? |
| kamāāk. | across, |
| asāāk. | on the other side. |
| Mâle, | Mary. |
| weoos. | meat, flesh. |
| mebet. | a tooth. |
| nebet. | my tooth. |
| kebet. | thy tooth. |
| webet. | his tooth. |
| wŏkŭn. | a knife. |
| sesĭp, | a bird. |
| abe, | a bow. |
| aabe. | a net |
| kadoo. | but. |
| mŭdŭ, | because. |
| wĕgĕt. | these. |
| tĕgĕn ? | which ? |
| tan. | who, when. |

| | |
|---|---|
| Tooma, | Tom. |
| wĭktŭm, | I like the taste of it |
| wĭktŭk, | he likes the taste of it. |
| lōk, | very, greatly. |
| tĕlsŭm, | I cut it so. |
| tĕlsŭk, | he cuts it so. |
| tĕtāāl, | in that direction. |
| tĕltāām, | I chop it so. |
| nĕgŭm, | be, she, him, her. |
| neloo, | my food. |
| keloo, | thy food. |
| weloo, | his food. |
| keele, | it is thou. |
| Pol, | Paul. |
| Peāl, | Peter. |
| Cătlĭn, | Catharine. |

---

## LESSON 6.

| | |
|---|---|
| Uchkeen, | My brother, (*younger than I*). |
| 'Nsees, | My brother, (*older than I*). |
| Nŭmees, | My sister, (*older than I*). |
| 'Nkwājech, | My sister, (*younger than I*). |
| nagoo'sĕt, | the sun. |
| dĕpkĭk, | the night |
| naagwĕk, | the day. |
| dĕpkŭnoo'sĕt, | the moon ; a month. |
| astaak, | the sun comes out. |
| astĕk, | the sun is out. |
| chiktĕk, | all is still: silence reigns. |
| āwĭpk, | the sea is calm. |
| stŭgā', | like: so as. |

| | |
|---|---|
| memā, | oil, fat (*of any kind*). |
| kŭmoo, | a cake of tallow, |
| mŭnow, | the fat of a bird. |
| oosŭk, | the fat on the kidneys. |
| Seboo, | a river. |
| kĕloo'lk, | pretty; good. |
| boose, | I go away by water. |
| boosĭn, | you go away by water. |
| boosĭt, | he goes away by water. |
| booseekw, | { we all go away by water, one canoe). |
| ĕdŭ, | if; perhaps ; it is so that. |
| boosoolteekw, | { we all go away by water, several canoes). |
| Kwedŭn, | a canoe. |
| 'ntool, | my canoe; my *ship*. |
| ootool, | his canoe. |
| ŭktool, | your canoe. |
| Ulŭmoo'ch, | a dog. |
| 'nte, | my dog. |
| ŭkte, | thy dog. |
| ooteel, | his dog. |
| kĕlpĭlk, | I tie him up. |
| kĕlpĭlt, | you tie him up. |
| kŭlbĭl. | tie him up. |
| sŭm, | feed him. |
| ĕsŭmŭk', | I feed him. |
| sŭmădĕs', | I will feed him. |
| moo ĕsŭmâk', | I dont feed him. |
| ma sŭmâk', | I will not feed him. |
| ĕntoo. | I loose it. |
| kwelŭm, | I seek it |
| kwĭlk, | he seeks it. |

| | |
|---|---|
| kwelān', | hunt for it; seek it. |
| kwĭltĕs', | I will seek it. |
| ăp, ăpch, | again. |
| koondāoo, | a rock ; a stone. |
| koondŭl', | rocks; stones. |
| mâskwe, | birch bark ; a birch tree. |
| kŭmoo'ch, | A tree ; wood. |
| dĕmĭk, | the water is deep. |
| wĕchpā', | { my canoe, (or ship), is deep in the water. |
| wĕspā', | my canoe leaks, [lit. *I leak*.] |
| wĕspĕn', | your canoe leaks. |
| wĕspĕt', | his canoe leaks. |
| wĕspĕgeâk', | the " canoe " leaks. |
| moo wĕspow, | my canoe does not leak. |
| moo wĕspĕkw', | his canoe does not leak. |
| moo wĕspĕge-anook, | { the " ship " does not leak |
| Enkâtk', | he measures it. |
| nŭt, | this, that. |
| nŭt na, | that's it; all right. |
| kāooche, | I am cold. |
| ĕpse, | I am warm. |
| chĭpse, | I start suddenly. |
| hĭktām', | I yawn. |
| kĕchkwā', | I hiccough, (hĭkŭp). |
| ĕkskwe, | I sneeze. |
| nōgŭm, | I cough. |
| sāskwā, | I yell; I scream. |
| ĕdĕk. | it lies there. |
| ĕpsaak, | a heated [stone]. |
| ĕpsŭm, | I beat it |
| ĕpsŭk. | he heats it. |

| | |
|---|---|
| ĕssŭm. | I colour it. |
| keek, | your house ; *also,* it is sharp. |
| neek, | my house. |
| week, | his house. |
| mĕskeek, | it is big. |
| mĕskĭlk', | he is big. |
| mĕlkāāk, | it is hard. |
| kâkkāāk, | it is rough. |
| kâkchĕk', | it is brittle. |
| sebĭk, | it is tough (tŭf). |
| ŭscŏŏs', | a weazle. |
| pāsk, | shoot him. |
| tŭleaa, | although. |
| moo chepalâk', | I don't fear him. |
| nŭgāā, | now. |
| pasŭk, | only. |
| chepălk', | I fear him. |
| mooĭn, | a bear. |
| wokwĭs, | a fox. |
| apchoo, | always. |
| nāāgow, | continually; all along. |
| wĕlămk, | { I like his looks; he seems pretty to me ; [lit., *I see him (or her) to be pretty.*] |
| mĕlooĭch', | especially. |
| koolkwes, | a pig. |
| kĕsălk', | I love *him* or *her*. |
| ootoon', | his mouth. |
| welnoo, | his tongue. |
| kelnoo, | your tongue. |
| nelnoo, | my tongue. |
| melnoo, | a tongue. |
| wĭlneel, | birds' tails. |

| | |
|---|---|
| wĭlne, | a bird's tail. |
| oosoogoone, | a beast's tail. |
| wĕltaak, | it is sweet sounding. |
| wĭntaak, | it is ill sounding. |
| amŏŏch', | certainly. |
| wĭkpŭk, | I like the taste of him. |
| wĭkpŭt, | you like the taste of him. |
| wĭkpăjŭl, | he likes the taste of him. |
| Pasŭk, | only, |
| ĕscŭpk', | I eat him raw, |
| escupt', | you eat him raw. |
| ĕskŭbŏŏl', | I eat thee raw. |
| Eskŭmāăgĕt, | he eats fish raw. |
| Eskemō' (Esquimeaux) | An eater of raw fish. |
| ĕksooĕt', | he tells a lie. |
| moo ĕksooow', | I dont lie. |
| ĕksooā', | I do lie. |

---

## LESSON 7.

Uchkeen, nagoosĕt nĕmeet ? 'Nsees, āā, nĕmeek: astaak ; astĕk : chĭktĕk, āwĭpk', stŭgā' memā'. Neen boose; keel boosĭn : ak Peāl boosĭt: booseekw: booseekw ĕdŭ ? mogwā'; boosoolteekw: kĕloo'lk seboo, kadoo dĕmĭk. Kadoo, pāl! kechka ; 'nte kĕlpĭlk': aa, ŭkte kŭl-bĭl': neen ĕsiimŭk' 'ŭkte.

Apch pāl! - kechka ; wŏkŭn ĕntoo ; wŏkŭn kwelŭm: keel kwelān': āā, neen kwĭltĕs': ak ĕlp 'nkwĭs kwĭlk, ak ŭkwĭs: coondāoo kwĭlk, ak maskwe, ak kŭmoo'ch.

Seboo dĕmĭk: āā, ŭchkeen, lōk dĕmĭk. San

ĕnkâtk' seboo.   Wĕspĕn ?   āā, wcspā', mŭdŭ
wĕchpā' : kadoo Peāl moo wĕspĕkw.   Coondāoo
ĕdĕk' : ĕpsaak.   Wĕn ĕpsŭk ?   neen ĕpsŭm.
Mogwā'; kŭmoo'ch ĕpsŭm ; kŭmoo'ch ĕpsŭm, ak
ĕlp ĕssŭm.   Kŭmoo'ch ĕdĕk, ak coondāoo, ak
wŏkŭn.   'Nsees, amooch' keek nŭt wŏkŭn ?
Uchkeen, amooch keek na wŏkŭn ; lōk keek.
Kadoo kŭmoo'ch mĕskeek, ak mĕlkāāk, ak
kâkchĕk : kadoo oola' kŭmoo'ch sebĭk.

Pāl! ŭscoos nĕmeek, ŭscoos chepălk: pāsk
ŭscoos.   ŭscoos tŭ nĕmeet ? mogwā', moo, na
ŭscoos : mooĭn na : mooĭn nĕmeek: pāsk mooin.
moo chepalâk' mooĭn, tŭleaa keel chepălt ŭscoos: kadoo nĕmeek nŭgāā pasŭk wokwĭs : kadoo
keel pāsk wokwĭs: keel chepălt wokwĭs, ak
ŭscoos: kadoo neen mogwā': neen wĕlămk
wokwĭs, ak ŭscoos wĕlămk, ak mĕlooĭch' mooĭn
wĕlămk. wokwĭs ootoon wĕltaak: 'nsees, mogwā': wokwĭs ootoon wĭntaak: koolkwes ootoon
wĕltaak. Uchkeen, mogwā': lōk wĭntaak. Kadoo
keel wĭkpŭt, ĕscŭpt. 'Nsees, āā, wĭkpŭk', ĕskŭpk.
Kadoo mogwā'; ĕksooā'.

---

## L E S S O N   8 .

| | |
|---|---|
| Boosool', | Good day. |
| wĕlegĭskŭk, | It is a fine day. |
| Baase, | sit down. |
| atlasme, | rest yourself. |
| Wĕdŭmāĭn ? | are you busy ? |
| Mogwā', | No. |
| moo wĕdŭmāu, | I am not busy. |

| | |
|---|---|
| Kenoodŭmooe | teach me |
| kechka | a little |
| ŭlnooeesĭmk. | Indian talk. |
| aa, meamŏŏch, | yes, certainly. |
| Kes kĭlchĕk' keel | can you count |
| ŭlnooeesĭmk? | in Indian ? |
| āā, meamŏŏch, | yes, certainly. |
| Wĕleâk', | very well. |
| kenoodŭmooe | teach me |
| ĕgĭlchĕmk', | the art of counting |
| Kĭlchĕ', | count thou. |
| Kĭlchĕkw, | *you two* count. |
| Kĭlcha'dĭkw, | *all of you* count. |
| Mogwā, | No. |
| nāooktājĭt wĕn | some one |
| kĭlchĕch | let him count |
| wĕgŭla' coondŭl, | these stones. |
| kedāān. | count—*read off.* |
| Nāookt, | one, I. |
| taaboo, | two, 2. |
| seest, | three, 3. |
| nāoo, | four, 4. |
| nan, | five, 5. |
| ŭs'oogom, | six, 6. |
| ŭlooĭgŭnŭk', | seven, 7. |
| oogŭmoolchĭn, | eight, 8. |
| pĕskoonădĕk. | nine, 9. |
| 'mtŭln, | ten, 10. |
| 'mtŭln chĕl nāookt, | eleven, 11. |
| 'mtŭln chĕl taaboo, | twelve, 12. |
| tābeâk', | it is enough. |
| kakŭyâk', | it is all gone. |
| Tas'ŭgŭl 'msĭt? | How many in all ? |

| | |
|---|---|
| Tās'ŭgŭl ĕdŭ, | so many. |
| Mogwā ; mă kedān' | No; count on. |
| āā, mā ĕgĭlchā' | yes, I count on |
| meesokoo | unto |
| tabooĭnskaak, | twenty. |
| Cadoo | but |
| tŭlooĕk | you would say |
| tabooĭnskaagŭl | twenty |
| cŏŏndŭl, | stones. |
| ak tŭlooĕk, | and you would say |
| tabooĭnskŭksĭjĭk, | twenty |
| pŭlĕsk', sesĭpk, | pigeons, birds, |
| cheenŭmook, | men, |
| ābĭjĭk, | women, |
| mĭjooajechk, | children, |
| kŭsnâ', | or |
| tanĭk pasŭk, | who only (whoever) |
| memăjooltĭjĭk, | are alive. |
| Tĕleâk'nŭt? | Is that so ? |
| āā, tĕleâk ; | yes, it is so ; |
| estooāgŭl | they differ |
| ŭksedoon | your language |
| ak 'nsedoon. | and my language. |
| Ulnooeesĭmk | In Indian |
| tĕlooā' | I say |
| nankŭl coondŭl, | five stones. |
| nankŭl soonŭl, | five cranberries. |
| kadoo nanĭjĭk | but five |
| ŭlbadoo'sk, | boys, |
| nanĭjĭk | five |
| pŭlĕsk'. | pigeons. |
| Ap kenoodŭmooe | Again teach me |
| weisĭsk, | the beasts, |

| | |
|---|---|
| sesĭpk, | the birds, |
| ak uktŭgĭk, | and others |
| oowesoonŭmooŏl'. | their names. |
| Aă, aa, nel'ŭmoos. | yes, certainly, my sister-in-law. |
| Koolkwees, | A pig |
| mălkotk', | he eats it. |
| wĕtkoolk'. | I prevent him. |
| senŭmkw, | a wild goose. |
| Kobet, | a beaver. |
| mălkomk, | I eat him. |
| Wejĕk, | a spruce partridge, |
| pulĕs', | a pigeon. |
| skŭmtook, | also. |
| tĕam', | a moose. |
| kloopske, | a murre. |
| kwemoo, | a loon. |
| alt, | some. |
| ĕdook, | like enough. |
| chĭptook, | perhaps. |
| tĕgĕnĭk | which of them are |
| weisĭsk? | beasts? |
| sesĭpk, | birds. |
| mooinâk', | bears. |
| Wŏpskw, | a polar bear. |
| Wŏpskook, | polar bears |
| kĭtpoo, | an eagle. |
| kĭtpoo'k, | eagles. |
| kĭtpoo's, | an eaglet |
| mĕskĭlkĭk, | they *two* are large. |
| mĕskĭlooltĭjĭk, | they are *all* large. |
| moo mĕskĭloo'k, | they *two* are not large, |
| moo mĕskĭloolteekw, | they a*ll* are not large. |

## L E S S O N  9.

Uchkeen, keel kes kĭlchĕk ? Cā! kĭlchĕ;
wĕgĕt' koondŭl' kedāān: aa: nāookt, taaboo,
seest, nāoo, nan. Nŭt 'msĭt ? āā, nŭt na, tābeâk':
kakŭyâk': pasŭk nankŭl coondŭl wĕg'ŭla: amooch', tŭldĕch na tĕt.   Ak ĕlp nankŭl soonŭl.
Soon wĭktŭm : nedăp, wĭktŭm, ak nel'ŭmoos wĭk-
tŭk.   Koolkwees mălkotk soon.   Mogwā', nedăp, neen wĕtkoolk' : kadoo wejĕk mălkotk', ak
pŭlĕs'; kadoo neen mălkomk' wejĕk', ak pŭlĕs',
ak koolkwees, ak senŭmkw', ak ĕlp kobet, ak
ĕlp team, ak ĕlp kloopske, ak mooĭn, ak ĕlp
wŏpskw.

Nedăp', pegwĕlkĭk wĭkpŭjĭk weisĭsk' ak sesĭpk'.   Cadoo wokwĭs' wĭkpŭt? mogwā', nedăp,
mogwā' wĭkpâk' wokwĭsŭ : moo mălkomâk'.

Cadoo, nedăp', sesĭpk' ĕdook' 'msĭt wĕgĕt?
Mogwā': moo 'msĭt - sesĭpk'.   Alt sesĭpk', alt
weisĭsk.   Tĕgĕnĭk' sesĭpk?   Tĕgĕnĭk?, wĕgĕt
wĕg'ŭla ĕdŭ: wejĕk, pŭlĕs', senŭmkwâk', kwe-
moo, kloopske, ak kĭtpoo.   Tĕgĕnĭk' weisĭsk'?
Team' na, ak mooĭn, ak koolkwees, ak wokwĭs,
ak kobet, ak wŏpskw.   Team mĕskĭlk' weisĭs,
ak ĕlp mooĭn mĕskĭlk, ak mĕlooĭch' wŏpskw.
Kadoo  wokwĭs ak kobet mogwā' mĕskĭloo'k,
moo mĕskĭloolteekw.

----

## L E S S O N   10.

| Nedăp, | Comrade, |
| boosool. | good day. |
| atlasme, | rest yourself. |

| | |
|---|---|
| Wĕlaĭn ? | are you well ? |
| āă, wĕlāe, | yes, I am well. |
| Wĕlāāk kooch ? | Is your father well ? |
| kechka wĕlāāk, | he is somewhat well. |
| ĕbĭt', | he sits (i.e., *he is at home*). |
| mā, māch, | still, yet. |
| kegooŏk', | at your house. |
| Tame wĕjeĕn ? | { Whence came you ? where are you from ? |
| Chebooktook, | from Halifax, |
| wĕjeā', | I come. |
| Tălāk ? | How is it ? how goes it ? |
| wĕlāāk, | it is well. |
| Wĕtkŭnāāk, | the weather is hot, |
| keskook, | to-day. |
| Tăl'eâk ? | What is the news ? |
| Tăleâk' ăgŭnood-ŭmâkŭn ? | { What is the news ? (what is true *as to the* news?) |
| oolagoo, | yesterday. |
| ĕskĭtpoo'kĕk, | yesterday morning. |
| eskĭtpoo'nook, | To-morrow morning. |
| nŏktŭmoo'p, | you did leave it |
| sabonook. | to-moorrow. |
| Tan, | When. |
| nŏk'tŭmŭn, | do you leave it |
| Nŏktŭm, | I leave it |
| nŏktŭmăp', | I left it |
| Eskĭtpoo'k, | In the morning. |
| Sĕtŭn, | Windsor. |
| Sĕtŭnook', | *at, in, or from* Windsor. |
| Sābei, | this morning. |
| ĕdĕk, | it lies there. |
| Cogooā', | What ? a thing, something. |

| | |
|---|---|
| cogooāāl, | what things ? things. |
| ŭkpŭtŭn, | your hand. |
| ŭkpŭt'ŭnk, | In your hand. |
| Moo kĕjedoo'n ? | don't you know what it is ? |
| moo kĕjedŏŏ', | I don't know what it is. |
| kĕjedŏŏ', | I know what it is. |
| kĕjeek, | I know who he is. |
| moo kĕjeâk', | I don't know who he is. |
| aptoon, | a staff. |
| ā'ŏŏmŭn, | you use it. |
| āŏŏm, | I use it. |
| pĕmaadoo, | I carry it. |
| wĕleâk', | It is well: all right |
| Kespŭnā', | I am tired. |
| wĕchkwaadoo, | I bring it. |
| Wĭskogwā' | black ash wood. |
| nuhsoon, | my load. |
| kuhsoon, | your load. |
| wuhsoon, | his load. |
| kĕscook, | it is heavy. |
| nĕmedŏŏ', | I see it. |
| wĕje-wājeet, | [where] from find you him. |
| wājedoon' | you find it |
| Nebŏŏkt', | The woods. |
| nebŏŏktŏŏk, | in the woods. |
| wĭskok', | A black ash. |
| agŭmok', | A white ash. |
| kŭnĕk', | a long distance off. |
| kamāāk, | { The other side (of a *river, valley, or plain,* &c.) |
| Asāāk, | { The other side (of a *hill,* or *wood,* &c.) |
| as'agook, | on the other side of a hill. |

| | |
|---|---|
| kākwāāk, | High up. |
| kāākwŏkw. | the hill top. |
| kāākwŏgŏŏk, | on the hill top. |
| ĕtle, | there. |
| wājeek, | I find him. |
| āhkĭk, | they are there. |
| poogwĕlkĭk | many. |
| nadāāl, | there. |
| kakŭmooltĭjĭk, | they stand. |
| poogwĕlk', | much. |
| ĕksooĕn', | you tell what is not true. |
| ek, | he would be there. |
| egaalŭch, | if you put them there. |
| tŭlpĭch', | let him be so, (*sit so*). |
| pĭsok', | he would have been there. |
| keg'ooŏk | your home. |
| nĭgŭnâk', | my home. |
| tan tĕt, | where. |
| ech, | let him be. |
| es, | he would be there. |
| tĕleâk', | it is true. |
| tan tĕlooĕn', | what you say. |
| kĕdoonpei' | I wish to go to sleep. |
| kĕdookse, | I am sleepy. |
| ĕlesmaase, | I lie down, |
| nĕbei, | I go to sleep. |
| toogeā', | I awake. |
| nĕmchaase, | I sit up, |
| kakŭmaase, | I rise up. |
| kakŭme, | I am standing up. |
| ĕbaase, | I sit down. |
| ĕbe, | I am sitting down. |

pool'tenĕch,   let us all be sitting down.
kumedaanĕcb.   let us all rise up.
pedaanĕch.    let us all sit down.

---

## LESSON II.

Boosool', nedap', piskwaa, baase, atlasme. Wĕlăĭn? āā, wĕlāe. Kooch wĕlāāk? kechka wĕlāāk nooch. Māch eblt kegooŏk? āā, māch ĕbĭt' nĭgŭnâk'.

Tame wĕj'eĕn? Chebooktook wĕjeā' Tălāāk? Wĕlāāk, wĕleâk'.

Nedăp', wĕtkŭnāāk keskook; wĕjeĕn keskook? Mogwā', oolagoo wĕjeāăp. Tan nŏktŭmŭn chebookt? oolagŏŏ' ĕskĭtpookĕk nŏk'tŭmăp. Sĕtŭn sĕbei nŏktŭm. Cogooā' nŭt .ŭkpŭtŭnk ĕdĕk'? moo kĕjedoo'n? mogwā': moo kĕjedŏŏ': ăptoon' na. Keel ā'ŏŏmŭn ăptoon'? mogwā': pasŭk pĕmaadoo: aa; tŭldĕch; wĕleâk'.

'Nsees, lōk kcs'pŭnā! wĭskogwā' wĕchkwaadoo: nuhsoon mĕskeek ak kĕskŏŏk. Nĕmedoo. Tame ĕtle-wājedoo'n wĭskogwā'? Nebŏoktŏŏk ĕdŭ ĕtlewājedooăp': kŭnĕk' kamāāk, ĕtlewăjeek wĭskok' as'agook. Poogwĕlkĭk tŭ māch āhkĭk nadāāl wĭskok' kakŭmooltĭjĭk? āā poogwĕlkĭk kakŭmooltĭjĭk: Nedăp', obŭleĕn', ĕksooĕn': wĭskok moo āŭmoo'k kāākwŏgook: āk kadoo: keel egaalŭch es. Tĕleâk' tĕlooĕn'; ak ĕlp māch keg'-ooŏk' egaalŭch, es. Wĕleâk': ech: tŭldĕch, kedookse; kĕdoonpei': ĕlesmaase, nĕbei.

# LESSON 12.

| | |
|---|---|
| Seboo, | a river. |
| ĕsĭtk', | it flows out |
| sāāsitk, | it flows every way. |
| pegwĕlkŭl, | many. |
| kogooāāl, | things. |
| pĕgesĭnk', | he comes. |
| Ulbadoo, | a big boy: a bachelor. |
| ŭlbadoos, | a boy. |
| ŭlbadooch | a little boy |
| ŭlbadoosees, | a very small boy. |
| Ankăptŭm, | I look at it. |
| Ulŭmoo'ch, | a dog. |
| ābĭt, | a woman. |
| ābĭtās', | a girl. |
| ābĭtāsees, | I little girl. |
| mĭjooajeech, | a babe. |
| wĕchkwaadŏk, | he brings it |
| pāsköwā'. | a gun. |
| kĕdooleā' | I wish to go |
| ăbe. | a bow. |
| aabe. | a net. |
| wo, | a pot. |
| ŭktŭgŭl. | other things. |
| kĕkoonk'. | she holds it, *or* he holds it. |
| oopŭtŭn. | his *or* her hand. |
| oopŭtŭnk, | in *his* hand. |
| boochkăjoo. | a birchen bucket. |
| iadŏksoon | a bucket. |
| asoon. | cloth. |
| wŏltĕs. | a wooden dish |

| | |
|---|---|
| sāskwĕt', | she screams. |
| tĕle-sāskwĕt, | she screams so. |
| papĭt | she is in play |
| nĕdowet', | he shouts : he holloos. |
| wĕskwĭmsk', | He speaks to thee. |
| tĕlĭmsk', | he tells thee. |
| wĕchkoo'nk, | he hands it to me. |
| kŭnejŭn', | your child. |
| nejŭn', | my child. |
| tăladĕgĕn' ? | what ails you ? |
| tăladĕgĕt' ? | what ails *him* ? |
| sooaal, | take him. |
| ŭlmaal, | carry him home. |
| Jĭksŭtāān, | listen to it. |
| noodâk', | I hear him. |
| nĕnoostâk, | I know his voice. |
| tĕlĭmk', | I tell him. |
| ankaptāān, | look! behold! look at it. |
| choogoonāān, | hand it to me. |
| choogoon', | hand him to me. |
| kāān, | thanks. |
| wĕlaalĭn, | { you do me a favor: (I am obliged). |

## LESSON 13.

Cogooā' nĕmedoon' ? Seboo nemedŏŏ' ak ankaptŭm tan tĕt sāāsĭtk'. Aa. Nŭt tĕt āleĕn ? āā, na tĕt kĕdooleā'. Nĭgŭmaach, na tĕt ĕlp neen kĕdooleā'. Cogooā' ankăp'tŭmŭn ? Pegwĕlkŭl kogooāāl: cheenŭm pĕgesĭnk' ak ābĭt, ak ŭlbadoo, ak ŭlbadoos, ak ŭlbadoosees ; skŭmtook ābĭtās', ak ābĭtăsees, ak ŭlŭmoo'ch. Tasĭjĭk wĕgĕt? oogŭmoolchĭn-tāsĭjĭk wĕg'ŭla.

Cheenŭm pāsköwā' wĕchkwadŏk: ŭlbadoos pĕmaadŏk kŭmoo'ch; Abe wĕjooow' ĕbĭt, ak aabe; ak ĕlp wo ĕbĭt.

Abĭt kĕkoonk' boochkăjoo oopŭtŭnk : wĕjooow' ladŏksoon ĕbĭt'; ak wŏltĕs' nĕgŭm wĕchkwaadŏk.

Pāl! jĭksŭtāān ! ankaptān', ābĭt sāāskwĕt' : cheenŭm nedowet'. Tăladĕgĕt ābĭt tĕlesāāskĕt' ? papĭt, ĕdŭ, pasŭk papĭt.

Cheenŭm wĕskwĭmsk, tĕlĭmsk: "kŭnĕjŭn kĕkoonk; kŭnejŭn sooaal, ŭlmaal kŭnejŭn:" āā, nedăp, noodâk ; kĕjeek, neelmoos na. Tĕlĭmk' nejŭn choogoon'. Kāān, wĕlaalĭn.

| | |
|---|---|
| Pĭbŭnŏkŭn, | Bread. |
| Sesmogŭn, | Sugar. |
| Săm'oogwŏn, | Water. |
| Pŭtāwā', | Tea. |
| Mŭlâgĕch', | Milk, |
| Căsteōme, | Molasses. |
| Amalĕgŭn, | Calico. |
| Dāpŭtăt', | A potato. |
| Sabăn', | Porridge. |
| Booktāoo, | Fire. |
| Booktāweâk', | It strikes fire. |
| Bootāwaasĭk, | It is burning. |
| Tŭmeegŭn, | An axe. |
| Pootăleāwā', | A Basket. |
| Lŭtkaamŏŏn, | An arrow. |
| Booktāwĭt', | A meteor. |
| Booktāwĭchk', | Rum. |

| mĕgobaak, | wine. |
| kowŏtkoobe, | spruce beer. |
| sămoogowŏkŭn, | drink. |

---

## L E S S O N  14.

| Oochoo'sŭn, | The wind. |
| Wĕjoo'sŭk, | The wind blows. |
| Wĕttŭk, | It blows from. |
| okwŏtŭnook', | the North quarter. |
| okwotŭn, | The north. |
| Tame wĕttŭk ? | Which way is the wind ? |
| okwŏtŭnook'. | Northerly. |
| oochebĕnook', | Easterly. |
| Utkŭsŭnook', | Westerly. |
| Upkŭdāâsŭnook', | Southerly. |
| S ŭnoo- sŏktŭnook' | South westerly. |
| Tĕglămsŭk, | It blows cold. |
| Tĕgāāk, | The weather is cold. |
| Tĕgegĭskŭk, | It is a cold day. |
| Aoolămsŭn, | { A squall of wind: a whirlwind. |
| Noo'sŭk, | A gentle cool breeze. |
| Nāoosŭk, | A cold draught ot air. |
| Nĕstăjĭk | do you understand them |
| Ulnoo'k? | The Indians ? |
| moolnĭm, | not much. |
| Nestăgĭk, | I understand them. |
| Ulnooeese, | I speak Indian. |
| Moo tŭlĭlnooeesu | I don't speak Indian |
| stŭgā' keel, | like you, |
| Nĕn'ŭmŭn | do you understand |

| | |
|---|---|
| weegădĭgŭn ? | A Book ? |
| Nĕnŭm, | I understand by *lookmg at it.* |
| Nĕstŭm, | I understand by *hearing it.* |
| Nĕnŭm weegădĭgun, | I understand a book, i.e. *I can read.* |
| Nĕstŭm ŭlnooeesĭmk, | I understand *Indian talk.* |
| Nĕstool, | I understand thee. |
| Nĕnâk, | I know him *by sight.* |
| Nĕnool, | I know thee *by sight,* |
| Nĕnât, | you know him. |
| Nĕnooĭn', | you know me. |
| Nĕstooĭn, | you understand me. |
| Nĕstâk, | I understand him. |
| Nĕstăse, | I understand myself, i.e. *what I am saying.* |
| Nĕstooĭjĭk, | They understand me. |
| Egedŭm, | I read it. |
| Keskedŭm, | I can read it: I have read it. |
| Moo keskedŭmoo, | I can't read it. |
| Māse-kedŭm, | I can't read it. |
| oola'. | this. |
| Agŭnoodŭm, | I tell news. |
| Agŭnootk', | He, she, or it, tells news. |
| Tan tĕleâk', | what is true. |
| Egedŭmool', | I read it to thee. |
| Kedŭmoŏltĕs', | I will read it to thee. |
| oogoopchŭk, | Soon. |
| Keskăjāe, | I am ready. |
| Keskăjāĭn ? | Are you ready ? |
| Jĭksŭtooe, | Listen to me. |

| | |
|---|---|
| Tĕlkedŭm, | I read it so. |
| Tălked'ŭmŭn ? | How do you read it ? |
| Talked ŭm ? | How do I read it ? |
| Tĕlkedŭm, | I read it so. |
| Wĕlkedŭm ? | Do I read it well ? |
| Aā, Wĕlked'ŭmŭn | yes, you read it well. |
| Nĕmeăjŭl, | He sees him. |
| Mooĭnâl', | A bear. |
| Ulbadoosŭl, | A boy. |
| Kĕkoonk', | He holds it in his hand. |
| Webetĭt, | { He has teeth: he is armed with teeth. |
| Ookwŭs'āwĭt, | { He has claws: he is armed with claws. |
| Alăjŭl, | He says to him. |
| Nĕmool, | I see thee. |
| Pāskool, | I shoot thee. |
| Chĭgŭmĭt', | He growls. |
| Chepălool', | I fear thee. |
| Moo chepălooloo. | I don't fear thee. |
| Kookwaalool, | I seize thee. |
| Mĕskĭl, | I am big. |
| Apchāje, | I am little. |
| Apchājĭn, | you are little. |
| Apchājĭt, | He is little. |
| Apchāch'k, | It is little. |
| Mĕlkĭgŭnei', | I am strong. |
| Aje-mŭlgĭgŭnei, | I am stronger. |
| moo ĕnkoodă, | than ; not like. |
| Nŭgoo', | Now then. |
| wooljâkŭ. | slowly. |
| pĕmeĕt'. | he walks. |
| wĭswĭgŭnĕmoot'. | he is conquered. |

| | |
|---|---|
| wĕledaasĭt, | he is very glad. |
| Mălcomool', | I eat you. |
| Ankwāăse, | Take care of yourself. |
| Kāā! | Come on! |
| Choogoo'yĕ, | Come to me. |
| Wĕchkooeĕt', | He is coming. |
| Pāskăjŭl, | He shoots him. |
| Nābaajŭi, | He kills him. |
| Ebĕdŏksĭt, | He groans. |
| Sĭktĕsĭnk', | He falls down. |
| Mĕskŭnădĕsĭnk', | He drops. |
| Wĭswĭgŭnĕmĭmk', | I am conquered. |
| Tĕladĕgā', | I do it. |
| Tĕladĕgĕn, | you do it. |
| Moo tĕĭadĕgow'. | I don't do it. |
| Moo tĕladĕgowŭn. | you don't do it. |
| Ukŭmoochŭm, | your club. |
| Tĕladĕgĕt', | He does it. |
| Tĕladĕgĕk', | It does it. |
| Tĕlamoo'k. | It is so fashioned. |
| Tĕlebooktāweâk', | It makes such a fire. |
| Booktāoo, | Fire. |
| Tokoo, | Then. |
| Nĕpk, | He is dead. |
| Nāp, | I am dead. |
| Nĕbŭn, | you are dead. |
| Nĕbei, | I sleep. |
| Toogeā', | I awake. |
| nĕboo'dĭjĭk, | They are dead. |
| Emtogwŏlsĭt, | He boasts. |
| Kĕspeadooksĭt, | { The story about him is ended. |
| Eged'ŭmŭn, | You read it. |

| | |
|---|---|
| Mā kedāān, | Read on. |
| Eksooögŭn, | { A "yarn:" a made up story. |
| Atookwŏkŭn, | A legend. |
| Mow wĕnŭl, | No one |
| Kĕspoogwalagool, | It deceives him not |
| Mooĭnāweesĭt, | { He talks bear-talk: he makes a noise like a bear. |
| Moo nĕdowĕk', | He don't talk. |
| Nĕdowā', | I talk, |
| Nĕdowĕn', | you talk. |
| Nedowet', | He talks. |
| Nĕmeăch', | when he sees him. |
| wĕsemoogwŏt', | he runs away. |
| Suhkedŭm, | I am tired of reading it. |
| Seweā, | I am weary. |
| Suhkwŏdŭm, | { I am tired of stopping there. |
| Sāwegŭnae, | I am weak and weary. |
| Kespŭnā', | I am tired. |
| Mălāe, | I am lazy. |
| Moo mălāu. | I am not lazy. |
| Sĕskwāe, | I am industrious. |
| Sĕsak'ŭse, | I am active, nimble. |
| Sĕsak'ŭsĭjĭk, | They *two* are active. |
| Sĕsakŭsooltĭjĭk. | They are *all* active. |

---

## LESSON 15.

Wĕjoo'sŭk Tame wĕttŭk? 'Nsees' okwŏt-ŭnook' wĕttŭk. Lōk tĕglămsŭk. Tĕleâk' tĕloo-ĕn, tĕglămsŭk ; tĕgāāk, tĕgegĭskŭk keskook

Nedăp', nĕstăjĭk keel ŭlnoo'k' ? Moolnĭm ;
āā, kechka' nĕstagĭk: kadoo moo tĕlĭlnooeesu
stŭgā kelow'. Kadoo nĕstooĭjĭk, ak nĕstagĭk ;
nĕstool ak nĕstooĭn.

Nĕn'ŭmŭn weegăd'ĭgŭn ? Aā, nĕnŭm; kes-
kedŭm. Kāā, kedāān oot weegăd'ĭgŭn. Agŭn-
ootk' tan tĕleâk. Aa, kedŭmooltĕs' oogoopchĭk
Keskăjaĭn ? âă, keskăjāe: jĭksŭtooe tan tĕlked-
ŭm. Meamooch', jĭksŭtool'.

" Ulbadoos nĕmeăjŭl mooĭnâl', ak mooĭn nĕmeăjŭl ŭlbadoosŭl. Ulbadoos kĕkoonk' pāsköwā',
ak mooĭn webetĭt, ak ookwŭsāwĭt. Ulbadoos
âlăjŭl mooĭnâl': " Pāl! nedăp, nĕen nĕmool':
pāskool!" Mooĭn chĭgŭmĭt, mooĭnāweesĭt,
ālăjŭl ŭlbadoosŭl: " moo chepălooloo: neen
mĕskĭl; keel ăpchājĭn: neen mĕlkĭgŭnei', ăje-
mŭlgĭgŭnei moo ĕnkoodā keelŭ. Mălkomooltĕs ;
nŭgoo' ankwāăse, kokwaalool." Ulbadoos ālăjŭl : " kā! choogoo'yĕ." Mooĭn āleĕjŭl, wooljâkŭ
pĕmeĕt. Ulbadoos pāskăjŭl, nābaajŭl. Mooĭn
wĭswĭgŭnĕmoot': mĕskŭnadĕsĭnk'. Ulbadoos
lōk wĕledaasĭt. Na kĕspeadooksĭt ŭlbadoosŭ, ak
kĕspeadooksĭt mooĭn: kĭtk kespea'dooksĭjĭk.
" Kāāskwŭ !" (" well done you ! ")

Aa, wĕleâk', kĕloo'lk weegădĭgŭn eged'ŭmŭn.
Kadoo moo tĕleanook ; pasŭk ĕksooōgŭn na.
Mŭdŭ kĕjedoo tan tĕleâk oochĭt mooĭn : mooĭn
moo nĕdowĕkw: mooĭn kĕjeek, seowwu nĕmeek, ak noodâk', nĕnoostâk: mooĭnāweesĭt,
kadoo; chĭgŭmĭt, ak ankwāăsĭt: chepalăjŭl chee-
nŭmool; nĕmeăch' wĕsemoogwŏt.

Aa, tĕleâk' tĕlooĕn. Mā āp kedāān. Mogwā'; Suhkedŭm nŭgāā.

## LESSON 16,

| | |
|---|---|
| Nĭgŭmaach, | My friend. |
| tame wĕjeĕn ? | where are you from ? |
| Nĭgŭnâk', | our home. |
| Tame ā'leĕn ? | Where are you going ? |
| Ukchegŭnk', | To town. |
| Tĕgĕn' | which |
| ŭkchegŭn' ? | town ? |
| Tĕgĕn ŭkchegŭn' ? | which town ? |
| Chebooktook, | Halifax. |
| Kĕskwowoolĕn', | { you carry a heavy load on your back. |
| Okoodā', | my friend. |
| kĕskwowoolā'. | { I carry a heavy load on my back. |
| Kĕskook, | it is heavy. |
| Pĕmooptoo, | I carry it on my back. |
| Pĕmooptoon', | you carry it on your back. |
| Pĕmooptŏk, | He carries it on his back. |
| Ankooöwâ', | Fur. |
| Wokwĭs, | A Fox. |
| Wokwĭswei', | A Fox skin. |
| Wokwĭsweik', | Fox skins. |
| Moochpĕchweik, | Mink skins. |
| Mooĭnăweik', | Bear skins. |
| 'Mtaĭk, | Beaver skins. |
| Keoonĭkeik', | Otter skins. |
| Kewĕsweik', | Muskrat skins. |
| Wĭjāādenĕch, | Let us go together. |
| Nĕnageie, | I am in a hurry. |

| | |
|---|---|
| Wĕdŭmāc, | I am busy. |
| Elmadoon', | you carry it home. |
| Aleāăp', | I went. |
| Elmadoo, | I carry it home. |
| Elmadŏk, | He carries it home. |
| Elŭmeă', | I go home. |
| Elŭmeĕn', | you go home. |
| Elŭmeĕt', | He goes home. |
| Weoos, | Meat. |
| Wokwĭswā'-weoos, | Fox meat. |
| Moochpĕchwā', | Mink meat. |
| Mooĭnāwā', | Bear meet. |
| Keoonĭkāwā', | Otter meat. |
| Kewĕswā', | Muskrat meat. |
| Teamwā', | Moose meat. |
| Kallebooā', | Carribou meat. |
| Uktŭk, | Another. |
| Uktŭgĭk, | Others. |
| Aptoogoolĭn, | you return from hunting. |
| Meamooch', | Certainly. |
| Aptoogoole, | I come from hunting. |
| Cogooā' oochĭt ? | { Why ? wherefore ? for what reason ? |
| Kĕloo'lk, | It is good. |
| Moo kĕloo'ltŭnook. | It is not good. |
| Kĕloo'sĭt, | he is good: he is pretty. |
| Mechĭpch', | It is used as food. |
| Mechĭpchāwā', | food. |
| Mechĭpchŭk | *They* are used for food. |
| Kĕdŭl ĕdook', | True indeed. |
| Sakŭmow', | A chief: a gentleman. |
| Sakŭmaaskw, | A chief's wife: a lady. |
| Pawŏtkŭl, | He wants them. |

| | |
|---|---|
| Tălaadŏk ? | What does he do with it ? |
| Wĕle-abănkŭtk, | He pays well for it. |
| Abănkŭdŭm, | I pay for it. |
| Abănkŭd'ŭraŭn, | you pay for it. |
| Abănkŭtk', | He pays for it. |
| Tŭleaa, | Although, though. |
| Mow wĕn, | No one. |
| Moo wĭktŭmook, | { he does not like the taste of it. |
| Malkotk', | He eats it. |
| Mow wĕn mălkodŭmook'. | } No one eats it |
| Nŭgāāch, | Now : at this time. |
| Saak, | long ago. |
| Sakawāāchăk, | { One of former days. An ancient Indian. |
| Sakawāāchkĭk, | The ancient Indians. |
| ŭlnooŏk'. | An Indian, *dead & gone*. |
| ŭlnoo, | An Indian, *now living*. |
| Wĭktŭksŭbŭnĕk', | He was fond of it. |
| Mălkotkŭsŭnĕk', | He ate it. |
| Tălowtĭk ? | What is the price of *it*? |
| Tălowtĭt ? | What is the price of *him* ? |
| Tĕlowtĭt, | *He* is worth *so* much. |
| Tĕlowtĭk, | *It* is worth *so* much. |
| Pasŭk, | Only. |
| Nĕkwtăgĭk, | one dollar. |
| chĕl akŭdeiĭk, | and a half. |
| Taboo-ăg'ĭgŭl, | Two dollars. |
| Nās-ăg'ĭgŭl, | Three dollars. |
| Nāoo-ăg'ĭgŭl, | Four dollars. |
| Usookŭm-tāsăg'ĭgŭl, | Six dollars. |
| Ellooĭgŭnŭk-tāsăg'ĭgŭl | Seven dollars. |

| | |
|---|---|
| Oogŭmoolchĭn-tāsăg'-igŭl. | Eight dollars. |
| Pĕskoonăddĕk-tāsăg'-ĭgŭl, | Nine dollars. |
| Mĕtlas-ăg'ĭgŭl, | Ten dollars. |
| Mĕgōdĭk, | *It* is dear. |
| Mĕgōdĭt, | *He* is dear. |
| Oolāās, | Oh that! it would be well. |
| Pegwĕleedĭch, | If there were many. |
| Ooskwāâk', | could I have. |
| Neen mĭl'āsĭk. | I would be rich. |
| Mĭl'āse, | I am rich. |
| Mĭl'āsĭn, | you are rich. |
| Mĭl'āsĭt, | He is rich. |
| 'Owwejāājĭjĭk, | They are scarce. |
| Sooĕl, | Almost |
| 'Msĭt tan tāsĭjĭk, | All of them. |
| Kakayĕdâk', | They will be all gone. |
| Kakayâk', | It is all gone. |
| Tooök'! | I could'nt say. |
| Elmeegŭnĭk', | Hereafter. |
| Mĕmăjooenoo'k, | People. |
| Wĕnooch, | A Frenchman. |
| Wĕnoochk, | Frenchmen. |
| Aglaseāoo, | An Englishman. |
| Aglaseāook, | Englishmen: the white people, |
| Uktŭgĭk | others. |
| Nĕgŭm, | He, She; Him, Her. |
| Kesoo'lkw, | Our Creator. |
| 'nchejakŭmĭch, | my soul. |
| ŭkchejakŭmĭjenâk'. | our souls. |

| | |
|---|---|
| Adagale-k', | A Bull-frog. |
| Adoo'dooĕch'-k, | A Red Squirrel. |
| Amălchoogwĕch'-k, | A Raccoon. |
| Amalegŭnŏkcheech-k, | { A Tortoise, (*a small kind.* |
| Anamanskāāch-k, | *A* Mole. |
| Bâktŭsŭm-ook', | A Wolf. |
| Chepĭchkaam-ook, | A dragon. *A* BOA ! |
| Cheechkĕlooāooch-ŭk, | A Sheep. |
| Cheechkĕlooāoo-cheech-k. | } A Lamb. |
| Chĭchowĕch'-k, | { A  " Peeper," a small species of frog. |
| Elne-mĭkchĭkch'-k', | { A Tortoise, (*a larger species.*) |
| Emkokchăjĭt, | A Toad. |
| Emkokchăjĭjĭk, | Toads. |
| Goolwaakw, | A Hooded Seal. |
| Goolwaagook, | Hooded Seals. |
| Keoonĭk-âk', | An Otter. |
| Keewĕsoo-k', | A Mtiskrat. |
| Kewĕsooch'-k, | A young Muskrat. |
| Kobet-âk', | A Beaver. |
| Kōbetāāch-k, | A young Beaver. |
| Koolkwees-ŭk, | A Hog. |
| Koolkoojĭch'-k, | A Pollywog. |
| Kâlebŏŏ'-k', | A Carribou. |
| Kâleboo'ch-k, | A young Carribou. |
| Kŭlloo-'k, | A Condor, (A " Roc") |
| Lŭntook-ook', | A Deer. |
| Măd'ooĕs-k, | A Porcupine. |
| Meaooch'-ŭk' | A cat. |
| Mĕstŭgepegăjĭt, | A Buffalo, (*solid ribbed,*) |

41

měgōdĭkw: pasŭk někwtăgĭk chěl akŭdeiïk.
Cadoo moochpěchwei' lōk měgōdĭt: nanăg'ĭgŭl
tělowtĭt. Oolās' poogwěleedĭch ooskwāâk', mĭl-
āsĭk. Cadoo keoonĭkei' tălowtĭt? Nāooăgigŭl
tělowtĭt. Kadoo sooěl kakayâk' ănkooöwā';
oogoopchĭk 'msĭt tan tāsĭjĭk weisĭsk' kakayědâk'.
Amooch', nedăp', ak ělp 'msĭt tan tāsĭjĭk memăjooenoo'k kakayědâk': ŭlnoo'k, wěnoochk,
aglaseāook, kŭndagwěchk, ak ŭktŭgĭk. Cadoo
Kesoolkw yăpchoo eedo, ak ŭkchejakömĭjenâk
ma yăpchoo 'npoodeekw, yăpchoo ehtâk woolōd
ĭktook kŭsnâ woonmăjōd ĭktook.
  Nĭgŭmaach, těleâk' tělooěnŭ.

| | |
|---|---|
| Boktăbŭlooe, | I start on a hunting expedition. |
| Wĭscomāāsā, | I creep on moose. |
| Nootkāāgooei | I hunt rabbits. |
| Nědooögwāāsi | I hunt porcupines. |
| Noodogwā', | I dig them out. |
| Nědoogoole, | I hunt. |
| Nědoomskwā' | I hunt beavers. |
| Kěskooskwā', | I hunt bears. |
| Nědooagwā', | I hunt seals. |
| Nebōsŭlei, | I hunt porcupines by night. |
| Něbāwĭsk, | A moonlight night. |
| Nebaase, | I travel by night. |
| Wŏsĭtpaak, | A light night. |
| Wěgăděsk', | Northern lights. |
| Kewŏsk, | Heat lightning. |
| Kâktoogwâk', | Thunder. |
| Kâktoogowĭk | It thunders. |
| Wŏsogwŏděsl | Lightning: It lightens. |

| | |
|---|---|
| Wostāoo, | Snow. |
| Pĕsâk, | It snows. |
| Kĭk'pĕsâk, | It rains. |
| 'Mkoome egaat. | It hails, (*ice comes*). |
| Wobĭch, | Round snow. |
| 'Msĭgŭn, | Sleet. |
| Mĕseegowĭk, | A silver thaw. |
| Fokwaaskutk, | A dry hard frost. |
| Kĕkpāwĭsk', | Dew. |
| Wŏstowtŭk, | White frost. |
| Cāwŏsk, | { A blown down piece of woods. |
| Kĕskoolkāāsĕt, | He treads heavily. |

# LESSON I 8.

## THE NAMES OF THE BEASTS, REPTILES, AND INSECTS.

(N.B. The letters separated at the end of each name by a hyphen, are to be joined to express the *plural*.)

| | |
|---|---|
| Weisĭs-k, | A beast. |
| Sesĭp'-k, | A bird. |
| Nŭmāch-ŭk, | A fish. |
| Choojĭch-k, | A reptile. |
| Abalpakŭmĕch'-k, | A striped squirrel, |
| Abĭstănāooch'-ŭk, | A Martin. |
| Ableegŭmooch'-k, | A Rabbit. |
| Abŭkcheloo-k, | A Skunk. |
| Abooksĭgŭn-k, | A Lucifee. |
| Abŭkchech'-k, | A Mouse. |
| Achkăjĭt, | A Male Carribou. |
| Achkăjĭjĭk, | Male Carribous. |

| | |
|---|---|
| Adagale-k', | A Bull-frog. |
| Adoo'dooĕch'-k, | A Red Squirrel. |
| Amălchoogwĕch'-k, | A Raccoon. |
| Amalegŭnŏkcheech-k, | { A Tortoise, (*a small kind.* |
| Anamanskāāch-k, | *A* Mole. |
| Bâktŭsŭm-ook', | A Wolf. |
| Chepĭchkaam-ook, | A dragon. *A* BOA ! |
| Cheechkĕlooāooch-ŭk, | A Sheep. |
| Cheechkĕlooāoo-cheech-k. | } A Lamb. |
| Chĭchowĕch'-k, | { A " Peeper," a small species of frog. |
| Elne-mĭkchĭkch'-k', | { A Tortoise, (*a larger species.*) |
| Emkokchăjĭt, | A Toad. |
| Emkokchăjĭjĭk, | Toads. |
| Goolwaakw, | A Hooded Seal. |
| Goolwaagook, | Hooded Seals. |
| Keoonĭk-âk', | An Otter. |
| Keewĕsoo-k', | A Muskrat. |
| Kewĕsooch'-k, | A young Muskrat. |
| Kobet-âk', | A Beaver. |
| Kōbetāāch-k, | A young Beaver. |
| Koolkwees-ŭk, | A Hog. |
| Koolkoojĭch'-k, | A Pollywog. |
| Kâlebŏŏ'-k', | A Carribou. |
| Kâleboo'ch-k, | A young Carribou. |
| Kŭlloo-'k, | A Condor, (A " Roc") |
| Lŭntook-ook', | A Deer. |
| Măd'ooĕs-k, | A Porcupine. |
| Meaooch'-ŭk' | A cat. |
| Mĕstŭgepegăjĭt, | A Buffalo, (*solid ribbed,*) |

| | |
|---|---|
| Mĕstŭgepegăjĭjĭk, | Buffaloes, |
| Mĭkchĭkcb-ŭk, | A Tortoise. |
| Moochpāāch-k, | A Porpoise. |
| Moochpĕch'-k, | A Mink |
| Mooĭn-âk', | A Bear. |
| Mooĭnāāch-k, | A Cub. |
| Moonŭmkwĕch'-k, | A Woodchuck. |
| 'Mtaakw, | A Female Hooded Seal. |
| 'Mtaagook, | Female Hooded Seals. |
| Najŭmooktâkŭnĕch-k, | A Bat. |
| 'Mtāāskŭm-ook, | A Snake. |
| Mtâkooow', | A great black Snake. |
| Mtâkooŏk', | Snakes. |
| Năbeaakw, | A Male Seal. |
| Năbeaagook, | Male Seals. |
| Năbĕskw, | A Male Bear. |
| Năbĕskook, | Male bears. |
| Năbĕsŭm-ook, | A Male Dog. |
| Noosĕskw, | A Female Bear. |
| Noosĕskook, | Female Bears. |
| Pŭgŭmŭch'-k, | A Land Lizard. |
| Petăloo-'k, | A Lion. |
| Sâkskadoo-k', | A Flying Squirrel. |
| Sămoogwŏneech-k, | A Frog. |
| Skwāaakw, | A Female Seal. |
| Skwāaagook, | Female Seals. |
| Skwĕsŭm-ook, | A Female Dog. |
| Tâktalok', | { A Water Lizard (*Plur.* the *same*). |
| Tā'sebo-kw, | *A* Horse. |
| Tāābŭlch-ŭk, | A Goat. |
| Team'-ook, | A Moose. |
| Teamoo'ch-k, | A Moose Calf. |

| | |
|---|---|
| Uchkoolch'-ŭk, | A Frog. |
| Ulŭmoo'ch-ŭk, | A Dog. |
| Ulgwĕdook, | A Female Moose: a Cow. |
| Upkŭmk-ŭk, | A Fisher. |
| Uskoos'-k', | A Weazel. |
| Utkogwĕch-k, | A Wild Cat. |
| Wĕnjoo-team'-ook, | { An Ox or Cow, (Lit. *A French Moose*) |
| Wokwĭs-k, | A Fox. |
| Wŏspoo-k', | A Seal. |
| Wŏpskw, | A Polar Bear. |
| Wŏpskook, | Polar Bears. |
| Yăp-âk, | A Male Moose: a Bull. |
| Negeăjook, | A yearling Moose. |
| Nĭk tooögŭnĕch'-k, | A two year old Moose. |
| 'Nsogŭnĕch'-k, | A three year old Moose. |
| Oolâkŭnanāās-k, | A four year old Moose. |

(N. B. The age of the Moose is kriown by his antlers.)

| | |
|---|---|
| Cŭjebancheech-k, | { *A.* Beaver of the first year (*youngest litter*). |
| Peewech-k, | { A Beaver of *second* oldest litter. |
| *Pŭlŭmskw'-ook, | { A Beaver of the *third* oldest litter. |
| Ntooāām-k, | { My *tame animal, beast* or *bird*. |
| Aglaseāwāāsŭm-ook', | { An animal, owned by a white man. |

---

* *Note.— Three.litters* remain in the " House " with the old ones. The *oldest* are then turned off to "set up" for themselves.

| | |
|---|---|
| Ulnooāāsŭm-ook, | { An *Indian* Dog, *or any other kind of animal* |
| Teamoo-wāāsŭm, | { A Moose Dog, i.e., good at hunting Moose. |

---

## LESSON 19.

### NAMES OF THE BIRDS.

| | |
|---|---|
| Sesĭp-k, | A Bird. |
| Năbāoo-k, | A Male bird. |
| Uskwāoo-k, | A Female bird. |
| Mŭlchŭgoo'e-ak, | An unfledged bird |
| Upskoo-'k, | { A bird that is shedding its feathers. |
| Pĕskwĭt, | He sheds his feathers. |
| Abŏkŭjĕch-k, | A Woodpecker, |
| Amălĭkchaajĭt, | A Cat Bird, |
| Amălĭkchaajĭjik, | Cat Birds. |
| Abâktoo'e-âk, | The great Auk. |
| Amkoomĭnk-âk', | The Curlew, |
| Apchechkŭmŏŏch'-k, | The Black Duck. |
| Antawāās-ŭk, | The Black Woodpecker, |
| Booŏĭn-âk, | { (The Wizard), a small yellow bird. |
| Chĭgŭdŭleegĕch'-k, | The King-fisher. |
| Chĭjeechkwĕch-k. | { A species of Plover, a Beech Bird. |
| Chĭpchowĕch'-k, | The Robin. |
| Chĭjooegadĕch-k, | The yellow legged Plover |
| Amjabōkch-ŭk, | The Sea Pigeon. |
| Aldoksaneĕch'-k, | The Stone Plover. |

| | |
|---|---|
| Booktāoo-cheejĭt, | { A small-flame coloured |
| Chegonāmajeejĭt, | The " Topnot." |
| Chĭgŭj!ch-k, | The Speckled Plover. |
| Chĭkchowegŭnāāsecs-k, | { A small species of grey duck. |
| Chŭgeegĕs-k, | The Chickadee. |
| Kaktŭgabŭncheech-k, | { (The *Little Thunderer,*) The Chimney Swallow. |
| Kĕskeskoonăjĭt, | The Puffin ( *Wide nose*). |
| Kĕskeskoonăjĭjĭk, | Puffins. |
| Kaakakŏŏch'-k, | The Crow. |
| Kaka-wegĕch-k, | The Pigeon Duck |
| Kasgălĭgŭnĕch'-k, | The Nightingale. |
| Keasees-k, | A small Grey Gull. |
| Keneskwŏtkeĕch'-k, | The Grosbeak. |
| Keokwāām', | The Yellow Hammer. |
| Kegŭleegwĕch-k, | The Hen. |
| Kĭgŭlăgwĕch'-k, | { The Downy Woodpecker. |
| Kĭtpoo-k', | The Eagle. |
| Kĭtpoos-k, | An Eaglet. |
| Kloopske-ăk, | The Murre. |
| Kokŭjŭmooch'-k. | The Cuckoo. |
| Kookoogwĕs-k, | The Owl. |
| Kŭlogeĕch'-k, | The Swamp Robin. |
| Kopkĕch-k, | The Saw-whet. |
| Kŭdooŏboo-k, | The Shag. |
| Kwĕdădowwe-k, | The Pigeon Hawk. |
| Kwemoo-k', | The black lake Loon. |
| Kwemoo's-k, | A young Loon. |
| Kŭlokŭndeĕch'-k, | The Gull |

| | |
|---|---|
| 'Mtakooaagĕjĭt, | { The Toad Hawk, (*The killer of black Snakes,*) |
| 'Mtakooaagĕjĭjĭk, | Toad Hawks. |
| Magwĭs'-k, | The " Scape-grace." |
| Maktotpăjĭt, | The Blackheaded Gull. |
| Mălsĭkws-ŭk, | The wood Duck. |
| Mĕgobāoo-k, | The Fulmar Petrel. |
| Megobāoo-cheech-k, | The Stormy Petrel. |
| Mogŭlaweech-k, | The Brant Goose. |
| Mĭkchăgōgwĕch-k, | The Meat Hawk. |
| Mĭledow', | The Humming Bird. |
| Mĭledâk', | Humming Birds, |
| Măktāweakŭsĭt kĭtpoo. | The Ospray. |
| Maktāweakŭsĭt, | A dark grey Gull. |
| 'Mkŭdōpskoon-k, | { A large black backed Gull. |
| Mâktāwāāk abōkŭj-ĕch-k, | { The Ivory-billed wood-pecker. |
| Mŭgāĭktā'-āk chĭjech-kwĕch-k. | } The Land Plover. |
| Mĭgoonaasĭt, | { The Peacook, (*the out-spreader.*) |
| Mooe-âk', | The Sea Duck. |
| 'Mskegooeāās-k, | The Sparrow. |
| 'Mtāskŭmooāgĕjĭt, | { The "Snake-killer," (*A species of hawk.*) |
| Nanamĭkteĕs'-k, | The Sand Piper. |
| Nĭktoolnĕch-k, | The Forked-tailed Gull, |
| Năbāoo-k, | A male bird. |
| Nŭmŭtkŭlnāās-k, | The Wren, (Cocktail.) |
| Nowskĭpkamaalow-k, | The Bobolink. |
| Nebeāāch-k', | A small yellow bird. |

| | |
|---|---|
| Nikchĭpkŭdāāgĕdāoo-k, | The Ground-robin, (Lit *the leaf rattler.*) |
| Oonŏkpŭdeĕgĭsoo-k', | The Snipe : The Wood-cock. |
| Ooloogoone-ek, | The Yellow-hammer. |
| Ootkĭgŭnŭsees-k, | The Bull-bird. |
| Owŏntāāgĕjĭt, | The striped Woodpeck-er. |
| Poogootŭleeskeĕch-k, | A Blackbird. |
| Pechkwĕch-k, | The Night-hawk, |
| Pepoogwĕs'-k, | A Hen-hawk. The Swallow. |
| Poogwŏlĕs'-k, | The Cormorant. |
| Pŭjoo-k', | The Wild Pigeon. |
| Pŭlĕs-k, | The Partridge, The Sparrow-hawk. |
| Pŭlowĕch'-k, | The Teal, (a small spe-cies. |
| Pepoogwāāsees-k, | |
| Poogwāsees-k, Sĭktāgĕdāoo pepoog-wĕs, | *Lit.* the Smiter-hawk, (a large bluish species of hawk that kills its prey with a blow with its breast bone.) |
| Sesip-k, | A Bird. |
| Senŭmkw-âk'. | The Wild-goose. |
| Tĕdâkŭmĭkch'-ŭk, | A large species of Plo-ver, with *black legs.* |
| Tŭmaagune-âk, | The Shell-bird, (a species of duck.) |
| Tădagoo'-k, | The Gannet. |
| Tăgŭleech-k, | The Tame-goose, (*The Scolder.* |
| Tăgŭleeses, | The Gosling. |

| | |
|---|---|
| Teteĕs'-k, | The Blue Jay. |
| Tĕdâkĭl koo n e-âk'. | The king-bird. |
| Tetŭgŭle-âk', | The Horned Owl. |
| Tŭmgwŏlĭgŭnĕch-k, | The Crane, (*the Heron.*) |
| Ukchŭgwĕch-k, | The Teal, (a pied duck.) |
| Ulnâkŭneech-k, | A small duck, loon. shaped. |
| Ukchĭgŭ moo'eĕch - k, | The Coot. |
| Ukchekakakoo-k, | The Raven. |
| Uksene-âk', | The Grey Hawk. |
| Ukwtădăgoo-k', | The Gannet. |
| Umjăbōkch-k, | The Sea-pigeon. |
| Weŭkŭjŭmĕch'-k, | A Bittern. |
| Wĭskŭmagwăāsoo'-k,. | The Fish-hawk. |
| Wŏbŭlotpăjĭt, | The Bald Eagle. |
| Wŏbŭlotpăjĭjĭk, | Bald Eagles. |
| Wŏbe-kookoogwĕs-k, | The White Owl. |
| Wĕdāwlskŭdăt, | The Chipping Bird. |
| Wĕdāw!skŭdaadĭjĭk, | Chipping birds. |
| Wĭkweleĕch'-k. | The Whip-poor-will. |
| Wŏbesĭk'w-âk', | The Shell-drake. |
| Wejĕk-âk', | The Spruce Partridge. |
| Wĕlawāāch-k, | The Schreech Owl. |
| Wenjooe-pŭlĕs-k. | The tame pigeon, (Lit. The French pigeon.) |
| Wĕnjooe-pŭlowĕch-k. | The hen, (French partridge.) |
| Wĕnjooe-ăpcheech-kŭmooch-k, | The Tame Duck. |
| Weegădĭgŭnaak, | A White Gull, tipped black. |
| Wŏbe-âk, | The Swan. |
| Wŏbekwemoo-'k, | The white sea-loon. |

| | |
|---|---|
| Wobĕdâkŭnāoocb-ŭk, | The white-necked coot. |
| Wŏbĭlkoon-eâk', | The white-winged coot. |
| Wŏbe-ăpcheechkŭm-ooch-k. | } The Pied duck. |
| Wŏbe-senŭmkw-âk, | The white wild-goose. |
| Wŏbeteetŭgŭle-âk', | The white horned-owl. |
| Wŏdŏpcheejĭt | A small Yellow Bird. |

---

## L E S S O N   2 0 .

| | |
|---|---|
| Nĭkskam, | God. |
| Sāsoo Goole, | Jesus Christ. |
| Wĕstowoo'lkw, | Our Saviour. |
| Kesoo'lkw, | Our Creator. |
| Wasok, | Heaven. |
| Moosĭkoon, | The Sky. |
| Mŭnkwŏnaasĭk, | There is a rainbow. |
| Mŭnkwŏn, | A Rainbow. |
| Kŭlokowĕch'-k, | A Star. |
| Utkŭbok' | { A spring, (in summer time.) |
| Kesoobok' | A spring, (in winter time) |
| Alook, | The Clouds. |
| Moosegĭskw', | The air. |
| Moosegĭskŭdook', | Up in the air. |
| Makŭmegāoo, | The Earth. |
| Oosĭtkŭmŏŏ', | The World. |
| Ukchĭgŭm, | The Sea. |
| Mŭn'egoo, | An Island. |
| Elmĭktŭk'ŭmĭk, | { A Continent: the Main-land. |
| Ansălăwĭt, | An Angel |

| | |
|---|---|
| Mŭndoo, | The devil. |
| Mŭndooage, | Hell. |
| Hĕgŭndeāwĭmk, | Sunday. |
| Uktlămsŭtoookŭn, | Faith. |
| Oosŭtōgŭn, | Salvation. |
| Woolōde, | Happiness, |
| Wĕnmăjōde, | Misery. |
| Alasoodŭmâkŭn, | Prayer. |
| Uktabĕgeâkŭn, | A song. |
| Alasoodŭmei', | I pray. |
| Kĕdabĕgeā', | I sing. |
| Atlasmoode, | Rest. |
| Atlasmoode-gĭskŭk, | { The Sabbath : *the Day of Rest.* |

THE NAMES OF THE FISHES.

| | |
|---|---|
| Nŭmāāch-ŭk, | A Fish. |
| Năbĕmĕkw, | A male fish. |
| Skwĕmĕkw, | A female fish. |
| wesoon, | A name. |
| oowesoonŭmooŏl, | Their names. |
| Abodawaajĭt, | The Toadfish. |
| Anagwāāch-k, | The Flounder. |
| Adogwaasoo-'k, | The Trout. |
| Ajogoolooĕch'-k, | The Perch, |
| Amlŭmĕkw, | The Mackerel. |
| Amlumâk', | plur. Mackerel. |
| Angadaalow, | The Muscle. |
| Angadaalâk, | Muscles. |
| Agoogŭmekw, | The Herring. |
| Agoogŭmâk, | plur. Herring. |
| Amjĕlagwĕch-k, | The Minnow. |
| Alĭtkwaajĭt, | The Wake-fish. |

| | |
|---|---|
| Agŭdeĕbĭs-k, | The Sea-porpoise. |
| āās-ŭk, | The clam. |
| Boogŭnŭmowās-ŭk, | The Quahaug. |
| Bootŭp-âk', | The Whale. |
| Banogopskŭnow', | The Rock-eel. |
| Chegaoo-k, | The Bass. |
| Châgĕch-k, | The Lobster. |
| Chĭgŭjĭch-k, | The Periwincle. |
| Comkudamoo-'k, | The Sturgeon. |
| Eepmaajit, | The Sunfish. |
| Kaat, *plur.* kâdâk, | The Eel. |
| Kadōnoks-ŭk. | The Conger-eel, |
| Kagwĕt, *plur.* kagwĕdŭl. | { The Starfish : also, the Sea-egg. |
| Kĕgŭnălooĕch'-k. | The Skate, |
| Komkwĕch'-k, | The Sucker. |
| Keneskoonĕch'-k, | The Swordfish. |
| Kopskwĕdŭm-oo'k, | The Lamper-eel. |
| Kâkpĕsow', | The Smelt. |
| Kâkpĕsâk', | Smelts, |
| Kŭlok-wâk', | The Sculpin. |
| Kŭmĕkwsĭs-k, | The Lump-fish. |
| Moochpāch'-k', | The Porpoise. |
| 'Msanĕkw-âk'w, | The Halibut. |
| Mŭnăpskwĕs'-k, | The Chub. |
| 'Msamoo-k', | The Shad. |
| 'Mtăbĕs'-k, | The Mud-catfish. |
| 'Mtâksunch-uk, | A Lake-trout, |
| Năbetŭlĕch'-k, | A Male Salmon. |
| Nāglbetŭlow', | The Hake. |
| Nāgăbetŭlâk, | *plur.* Hakes. |
| Noogĭlchŭgĕch-k, | { A Lobster that has shed its shell. |

| | |
|---|---|
| Nŭmjĭnegĕch'-k, | the Crab. |
| Nŭmdŭmoo-'k, | The Oyster. |
| Pĕjoo-'k, | the Cod. |
| Pĕstŭm-oo'k, | the Pollock. |
| Poodomkŭnĕch'-k, | The Haddock. |
| Pŭlămoo-'k, | The Salmon. |
| Poonămoo-'k, | The Tomcod. |
| Săbŭdeemĕkw, | The Grampus. |
| Săbŭdeemâk', | Grampuses. |
| Sasăp, *plur.* Sasabâk', | The Jelly-fish. |
| Sasabĕgwĭt', | The Razor fish. |
| Sasabĕgwĭdŭl, | *plur.* Razor fish. |
| Sĕdaasoo-'k, | The Squid. |
| Sakskalāās-ŭk, | The Scallop. |
| Sebooāās-ŭk, | The freshwater clam. |
| Segoonŭmĕk'w, | The gaspereau. |
| Segoonŭmâk', | Gaspereaux. |
| Sĭgŭlăde-ek, | The Dogfish. |
| Sogŭmoo'ch-ŭk, | The Gudgeon. |
| Takooŏnow'; Takoo-ŏnâk', | The salmon-trout. |
| Tĕdmŭnătpăjĭt, | The Blackfish |
| Tĕdmŭnătpăjĭjĭk. | *plur.* Blackfish, |
| Upkwāāk-ŭk, | A small round clam. |
| Utkĕsoo-'k, | A young gaspereau. |
| Utkōgwĕch-k, | The catfish. |
| Uskoo-'k, | The Leech. |
| Webetŭmĕkw' Webet-ŭmâk'. | The Shark, (the *tooth-armed fish.*) |
| Wŏbŭnumĕk'w Wŏb-ŭnŭmâk, *plur.* | The white Porpoise. |
| Wŏlŭmkwĕch'-k, | The Lobster. |

## LESSON 21.

| | |
|---|---|
| Săm'oogwŏn, | Water. |
| Wĭskŭbok', | Salt water. |
| Nkŭnōbăde, | A well. |
| Utkŭbok', | { A Summer-spring of water, (*cool water*). |
| Kesoobok', | { A winter-spring of water, (*warm water*). |
| Poolkŭjâkŭmeâk', | A boiling Spring. |
| Wostāoo, | Snow. |
| Pāsâk, | It snows. |
| Kĭk'pāsâk, | It rains. |
| Kâktoogwâk', | Thunder. |
| Kâktoogöwĭk', | It thunders. |
| Umkoome, | Ice. |
| Umkoome egaat, | It hails, (*ice comes.*) |
| Wŏsogwŏdĕsk', | It lightens. |
| Wŏsĕdĕk, | Light |
| Wŏpk, | It is day. |
| Wŏbŭn, | Daylight. |
| Wĕchkwŏbŭneâk', | Day dawns. |
| Bogŭnĭtpaak, | Darkness. |
| Meowlagwĕt', | Noon. |
| Aktatpaak, | Midnight. |
| Kĕsĭk, | Winter. |
| Togwaak, | Autumn. |
| Nĭpk, | Summer. |
| Sĭkw, | Spring,- |
| Naagwĕk, | Day. |
| Dĕpkĭk, | Night. |
| Eskĭtpoo'k, | Morning. |

| | |
|---|---|
| Wĕlaakw, | Evening. |
| Wĕleoolaakw, | A pleasant evening. |
| Amase-gĭskŭk, | A long day. |
| Amasĭtpaak, | A long night. |
| Amasebook', | A long winter. |

## NAMES OF TREES AND PLANTS.

| | |
|---|---|
| Ajeŏkchemanŏkse-el, | The Blackberry bush. |
| Aboodăpkeĕjĭt, | The Juniper. |
| Agŭmōk', | The white ash. |
| Alogomanokse-el, | The Grape-vine. |
| Chĭjĭkpe-el, | Leather-wood, |
| Cheŏkchemoose-el, | White Maple. |
| Elnĭkpe-el, | Bass-wood. |
| Egwĭtkāwāāl, | The "Chocolate" plant. |
| Gooö': Gooâk, | The White Pine. |
| Imkwŏlogŭm-ŭl, | A species of willow. |
| Kŭljemanŏkse-el, | Bayberry. |
| Kowĭksaak, | Thorns. |
| kagĭpk-ool, | The Honeysuckle. |
| Kadaskool, | Eel-grass. |
| Kâstŭk, | Ground-hemlock. |
| Kowĭksomoose-ek, | The thorn-tree. |
| Keŏkchemoose-l, | The White Maple. |
| Kagĭpkwŏkse-1, | Poison Laurel. |

* NOTE.—There are *two* Genders in Micmac, *viz:* the *Animate*, denoting objects having *animal life;* and the *Inanimate*, denoting inanimate objects. But many of the *trees* and *plants,* and some other inanimate objects, are treated as *animate,* and *verbs* and *Adjectives* are made to agree with them accordingly. Such words may be distinguished by ihe termination of the *Plural,* which has usually *k* for the *Animate,* and *l* for the *Inanimate.*

| | |
|---|---|
| Kŭlŭmooĕjemânŏkse-ek, | The Bilberry tree. |
| Kĭktŭgĭkooaak sŭnowā, | Curly maple. |
| Kadomĭnŏkse, | Swamp-raspberry bush. |
| Ketâkŭneraoose-l, | The Shumac. |
| Kenegwĕjĭt, | The thistle : the briar. |
| Kewĕswŏsk-ool, | The sweet-flag. |
| Kŭledōmoose-k, | Raspberry bushes. |
| Kowŏkchĕchkemoose-ek. | The Gooseberry bush. |
| Kajoo-'k, | An edible root. |
| Kajooemachkŭl, | Water-cresses. |
| Maskoosĭt-ŭl, | Ground-nuts. |
| (Maskoosĭtkĭk, | Name of the Isle of Haut) |
| Kŭledowĭpkŭk, | A medicinal root. |
| Kâkskoose-l, (also Sâkskoose-l,) | The Cedar. |
| Kowŏtk'w-ook, | The Red Spruce. |
| Kogŭmĭnŏkse-ek, | The Thorn tree. |
| Lĭpkŭdămoon-k, | The Lady's-slipper. |
| Looemanŏkse, | The choke-cherry tree. |
| Maskwe-el, | The White birch. |
| Maskwāse-manŏkse-el, | The Wild-cherry tree. |
| Malĭpkanchemoose-el, | The Hazel-nut bush. |
| Masoose-el, | Brakes. |
| 'Mskegool, | Grass. |
| Mĕkwskŭdăjĭt, Mĕkwskŭdăjĭjĭk, | The yellow Pine, |
| Mede-ek, | The Poplar. |
| Mĭmkwŏnmoose-el, | The Oak. |
| Mĭmkŭdowōk, | Moosewood. |
| 'Mtōp, | Moosewood leaves. |
| Nasoonŭl, | Rushes. |
| Nĭmnogŭn-k, | The Black Birch. |

| | |
|---|---|
| Nebe-ek, | Leaves. |
| Nebeel, | Cabbage. |
| Nĭbŭmânŏkse-el, | The bush-cranberry-tree |
| Nasoon-ŭl, | The rush. |
| Owĕlĭkch'-ŭl, | The Horn-beam. |
| Oojegŭnŭmoose-1, | The spotted alder. |
| Ootŭbe-ek, | A spruce root. |
| Pakŭnatkwemoose-1, | { Pipe-stem-wood, (a species of willow.) |
| Poogoolooskwemoose-1, | The Elder. |
| Poogoolooskw-ool, | Elder wood. |
| Pĭjĭstŭgwaalŭk, | { I smoke him out of a hollow tree. |
| Pĭjĭstŭkw, | A hollow tree. |
| Sŭmgwŏdĭgŭn-k, | Poison Flags. |
| Sĕsoo'sk-ool, | Reeds. |
| Sakskoose-ek, | The Cedar. |
| Sāoopogeăchk-ŭl, | The Grey Birch. |
| Sŭgĕbbŭn-k, | { The ground-nut, *or* Indian potato. |
| Sĭgŭlădeâskw'-ool, | Scouring-rushes. |
| Sooömoose-1, | The Beech. |
| Stokŭn-k, | The Fir. |
| Sŭnow, | The Rock-maple. |
| plur. Sŭnăl', | Rock-maples. |
| Toogemanŏkse-el, | Sheep-berry bush. |
| Toobe, & Toppse, | The Alder. |
| Alogomânŏkse, | A grape-vine. |
| Mesâkŭnâtkool, | Moss. |
| Nebeek, | Leaves. |
| Wosöwĕchkŭl, | Blossoms. |
| Menĭchkŭl, | Fruit. |
| Menĭchkŭl, | Berries. |

| | |
|---|---|
| Ulgĕdoo-'k, | A Mushroom. |
| Chegoksook, | Touchwood, |
| Upkwemânŏkse-ek, | The blueberry; bush. |
| Skŭnaaskw-ook, | The cat-tail flag. |
| Skŭnow', Skŭnâk', | The cat-tail flag. |
| Mĕnătkĕk, | A Grove. |
| Mŭnegooŏtkĕk, | A clump of tree's. |
| Nebookt', | The woods. |
| Nebooktook, | *In, at* or *from,* the woods. |
| Ulnogom-ŭl, | A *green* tree. |
| Mŭljogom, | A dry tree. |
| Ulnekŭmooch', | All species of hard-wood. |
| Oocheegŭch, | A stump. |
| Tŭmgoodeŭnskw, *plur.* Tŭmgoodeŭnskook, | A stub, *or* a broken tree. |
| Kooŏsŭn-k, | A wind-fall. |
| Tŭmoktaoo, | A log chopped. |
| Lămkĕsŭn-k, | A moss-covered log. |
| Wokŭnoo'jŭl, | Dry broken hard-wood limbs. |
| Nĕmăpskeâk-ŭl, | A rocky hill. |
| Uptāwokŭn, | A dead charred tree. |
| Uptāwokŭn-aagŭmĭkt, | A district of dead charred trees. |
| 'Mskegooāākăde, | A meadow. |
| Cogooā-aagŭmĭkt? | What kind of a grove is it? |
| Mĭmkwŏnmoose-aagŭmĭkt, | It is an oak grove. |
| Chekawŏbe-el, | Spikenard. |
| Pagōse-ek, | A lilly. |
| Tŭlĕgōbŭn-k, | Poison hemlock. |
| Kŭledow-maagāwā'-1, | Elecampane. |

| | |
|---|---|
| Kadonpesoon-ŭl, | Dock. |
| Wāĭpkŭchk-ŭl, | |
| Mâldāweŭchk-ŭl, | Bloodroot. |
| Upsĕskw-ool, | Mint. |
| Pŭlămooĭpkool, | Spearmint. |
| Wŏsooö', plur. wŏsooŏk', | |
| 'Mtăsok-ool, | A bluff. |
| Kŭskĭbŭnagĕk-ŭl, | A steep river-bank. |
| Mălĭkt-ool, | A hard-wood grove. |
| Nebookt'-ool, | A wood. |
| Kowŏtkwaagŭmĭkt-ool, | A soft-wood grove. |
| Nebesaagŭmĭkt-ool, | { A second growth of hard wood trees. |
| Upkwaoo, | Soft-wood bark. |
| Plur. of ŭpkwaoo, is, ŭpkwaak. | |
| Maskwe-el, | Birch bark. |
| Oochŭkŭl-maaskwe-el, | Hard-wood bark. |
| Nĕtkwĭkt-ool, | An interval. |
| 'Mkooögwŏtkĭkt-ool, | A black-spruce swamp. |
| Ooseogĭkt-ool, | A swamp. |
| 'Mkooök'-ool, | A bog. |
| Uptāwĭkt-ool, | A plain. |
| Wŏlāāk-ool, | A valley. |
| Cŭmdŭn-k, | A mountain, (*peak.*) |
| Pŭmdŭn-k, | A mountain, (*chain.*) |
| Pĭjĭskĭk. | A hollow hard-wood tree. |
| Pĭjĭstŭkw-', | The log or tree *is hollow.* |
| Oochebŭsk-ŭl, | A root. |
| Upsĕtkoon-ŭl, | A branch. |
| Ooskedogom, | Alburnum. The sap. |
| Lămogom, | The heart of a tree. |
| Booksook-ŏŏl, | Fuel. |
| Mĕgŭnsā', | I get wood for night. |

| | |
|---|---|
| Esnogŭnā', | I am picking up fuel. |
| Uchkoolchemoose-el, | (Frog wood): a species of Dogwood. |
| Ukchĭgŭmooŏtkw'-ook:, | The white Spruce. |
| Upsāmoose-el, | The Prickly Ash:"round-tree." |
| Umkwŏbĕkw Umkwŏbĕgool, | Red Willow. |
| Ulnâtkw, Ulnâtkook, | The Black Spruce. |
| Uksoo'sk-ŭk, | The Hemlock. |
| Upkwŏlĭgŭnŭmoose-1, | |
| Upsoolemanŏkse-el, | The Choke-berry bush. |
| Upkânemoose-1, | The Butternut. |
| Upskŭnâkŭnemoose, | The Withe-rod. |
| Wāgwŏnŭmanŏkse, | The Black Cherry tree. |
| Wĕnjoosoonŏkse, | The Apple tree. |
| Wŏbogom'-ŭl, | Dogwood, |
| Wĭskok, | The Black ash. |
| Wŏseboogooĭchk-ŭl, | A species of White Birch |
| Wĭkpe-el, | The Elm. |
| Mĕnpā', | I gather spruce roots. |
| Mĕnâstā, | I gather Fir boughs. |
| Wŏbabâkchŭk'ŭl, | Sarsaparilla. |

---

# LESSON 22.

| | |
|---|---|
| Kwāā! | Hail! . |
| Boosool, | Good day! |
| Okoodā', | My Friend. |
| Tăleoolăĭn ? | How are you ? |
| Moo wĕlāu, | I am not well. |
| Kechka wĕlāe, | I am " only so so." |

| | |
|---|---|
| Wĕlāe, | I am well. |
| Kĕsenookwŏn'? | Are you sick? |
| Kĕsenookwei', | I am sick. |
| Kĭgŭmanoo, | Our comrade |
| Mĭjooajech', | The babe |
| Kĕsenookwŏt', | Is sick. |
| Tălĭksenookwŏn? | What ails you? |
| Nŭnooche | My head |
| Kĕsenoogooĭk'. | pains me. |
| Koo'choode, | A cold |
| mătŭnĭk', | } Fights me, (i.e., *I have a cold*) |
| Wĕpskoonenā', | I have the consumption. |
| Wĕpskoonĕnĕn', | you have &c. |
| Wĕpskoonenĕt', | He has &c. |
| Tădoojĭksenookwŏn'? | How sick are you? |
| Tădoo-jĭpkĭjĭkse-noo-kwŏn'? | } How long have you been ill? |
| Taboosĭjĭk | Two |
| Dĕpkŭnoosĕjĭk, | Months. |
| Dĕpkŭnoosĕt, | The Moon.   A Month. |
| Mĕskăe, | I am sorry. |
| Wĕledaase, | I am glad. |
| Tasăj'eĕt? | What o'clock is it? |
| Tădoojenagwĕk? | What time of day is it." |
| Tălĭtăt'? | How high is the sun? |
| Tĕlĭtăt' | The sun is *so* high. |
| Naagwĕk, | Day. |
| Wŏsogwĕk', | Light. |
| Dĕpkĭk, | Night |
| Bogŭnĭtpaak, | Darkness. |
| Wŏbŭn, | Day light. |
| Sĕgāwaat, | Sunrise. |

| | |
|---|---|
| Eskĭtpoo'k, | Morning. |
| Eskĭtpoo'nook, | To-morrow morning. |
| Keskăjeboogooeĕt', | Middle of the forenoon. |
| Meowlagwĕt', | Noon. |
| Kĭpkwaat, | Middle of the afternoon. |
| Kŭlkwaseĕt', | Sundown. |
| Wĕlaakw, | Evening. |
| Oolonook, | The ensuing evening. |
| Aktatpaak, | Midnight. |
| Sĭkw, | Spring. |
| Segoon, | Last spring. |
| Segoonook, | Next spring. |
| Nĭbŭn, | Last summer. |
| Nĭpk, | Summer. |
| Nĭbŭnook', | Next summer. |
| Togwaak, | Autumn. |
| Utkōnook, | Next Autumn. |
| Utkōk, | Last Autumn. |
| Kĕsĭk, | Winter. |
| Uksĭn, | Last winter. |
| Uksinook, | Next winter. |
| Wĕlegĭskŭk, | It is a fine day. |
| Mĕdooegĭskŭk, | It is a foul day. |
| Mĕdooamoogwaasĭk, | The weather is stormy. |
| Oolegĭskŭk, | If the day be fine. |
| 'Mtooamoogwaasĭk, | If the day be stormy. |
| Magatkwik, | The sea is rough. |
| Wĭbŭn, | A calm. |
| āwĭbŭneâk', | It grows calm. |
| āwĭpk. | It is calm weather. |
| Chĭktĕk, | Silence reigns. |
| Pesāoo, | Froth, Foam. |
| Pesāootoonaat, | He foams at the mouth. |

| | |
|---|---|
| Pesāoo-oogwĕk, | It foams. |
| Pesāoo-wŏmkĭtk, | Water foams as it flows. |
| Cogŭn, | Scum of the sea. |
| Okokpĕgeâk', | Scum gathers on the water. |
| Okokŭyâk', | It grows mouldy. |
| Kâpskw, | A water-fall, a cascade. |
| Kuhkw, | An earthquake. |
| Tălooesĭn? | What is your name? |
| Sosĕp tĕlooese. | My name is Joseph. |
| Taseboonan'? | } How many years old are you? |
| Tădoojăĭn? | How old are you? |
| Mĕtlaseboonei', | I am ten years old. |
| Mĕtlaseboonei'  chĕl 'looĭgŭnŭk, | } I am ten years old and seven. |
| Tabooĭnskŭgeboonei', | I am twenty years old. |
| Tălooweedŭmŭn oot.? | What do you call it this? |
| Kwedŭn | A canoe |
| Tĕlooweedŭra, | I call it |
| Ulnooeesĭmk, | In Indian. |
| Aglaseāweesĭmk, | In English. |
| Ulnooeese, | I speak Indian. |
| Ulnooeesĭn, | you speak Indian. |
| Ulnooeesĭt, | He speaks Indian. |
| Ulnooeeseekw, | *you* and *I* speak Indian. |
| Ulnooeeseĕk', | *He* and *I* speak Indian. |
| Ulnooeeseŏk', | you *iwo* speak Indian. |
| Ulnooeesĭjĭk, | They two speak Indian. |
| Ulnooeesoolteekw, | you *all* and *I* speak Indian. |

| | |
|---|---|
| Ulnooeesoolteĕk', | { *They all* and *I* speak Indian, |
| Ulnooeesoolteŏk', | you all speak Indian. |
| Ulnooeesooltĭjĭk, | They all speak Indian. |
| Nĕstăjĭk ŭlnoo'k ? | { Do you understand Indian ? (Lit. *do you understand the Indians ?*) |
| Aā, nĕstagĭk, | { Yes, I understand them. |
| Mogwā', moo nĕstoo-agĭk, | No, I don't understand them. |

# LESSON 23.

## THE NUMERALS.

### EGILCHEMKAWAAL.

| | | |
|---|---|---|
| Nāookt, | One, | 1. |
| Taaboo, | Two, | 2. |
| Seest, | Three, | 3. |
| Nāoo, | Four, | 4. |
| Nan, | Five, | 5. |
| Us'ookom, | Six, | 6. |
| Ellooĭgŭnŭk', | Seven, | 7. |
| Oogŭmoolchĭn, | Eight, | 8. |
| Pĕskoonâddĕk, | Nine, | 9. |
| 'Mtŭln, | Ten, | 10. |
| 'Mtŭln chĕl nāookt, | Eleven, | 11. |
| 'Mtŭln chĕl taaboo, | Twelve, | 12. |
| 'Mtŭln chĕl seest, | Thirteen, | 13. |
| 'Mtŭln chĕl nāoo. | Fourteen, | 14. |
| 'Mtŭln chĕl nan, | Fifteen, | 15. |

| | | |
|---|---|---|
| 'Mtŭln chĕl ŭs'ookom, | Sixteen, | 16. |
| 'Mtŭln chĕl 'looĭgŭnŭk', | Seventeen, | 17. |
| 'Mtŭln chĕl oogŭmoolchĭn, | | 18. |
| 'Mtŭln chĕl pĕskoonâddĕk, | | 19. |
| Tabooĭnskaak, | Twenty, | 20. |
| Tabooĭnskaak chĕl nāookt. | | 21. |
| Nāsĭnskaak, | | 30. |
| Nāooĭnskaak, | | 40. |
| Nanĭnskaak, | | 50. |
| Usookom-tāsĭn skaak, | | 60. |
| Ellooĭgŭnŭk-tāsĭnskaak, | | 70. |
| Oogŭmoolchĭn-tāsĭnskaak, | | 80. |
| Pĕskoonâddĕk-tāsĭnskaak, | | 90. |
| Kŭskĭmtŭlnâkŭn, | | 100. |
| Kŭskĭmtŭlnâkŭn chĕl nāookt, | | 101 |
| Taaboo kŭskĭmtŭlnâkŭn. | | 200. |
| Seest kŭskĭmtŭlnâkŭn, | | 300. |
| Usookom' tās kŭskĭmtŭlnâkŭn, | | 600. |
| Betooĭratŭlnâkŭn, | | 1000. |

Taaboo kŭskĭmtŭlnâkŭn be-⎫
tooĭmtŭlnâkŭn.          ⎬ 200.000.

Ukchebetoo- ⎫ one million,   1.000.000.
ĭmtŭlnâkŭn ⎭

kŭsnâ'  mĕskeek  be- ⎫ or *the great thousand.*
tooĭmtŭlnâkŭn,        ⎭

---

| | |
|---|---|
| Pĭbŭnŏkŭn, | Bread. |
| Mŭlâgĕch', | Milk. |
| Mŭlagĕch'-weeme, | Butter. |
| Memā', | Oil, Fat, Grease. |
| Câsteōme, | Molasses. |
| Pŭtāwā', | Tea. |
| Tŭmawă', | Tobacco. |

| | |
|---|---|
| Tŭmâkŭn, | A Pipe. |
| Kwĕdŭmei', | I smoke. |
| Kwĕdŭmân', | you smoke. |
| Kwĕdŭmât', | He smokes. |
| Neen, | I, Me. |
| Keel, | Thou. |
| Nĕgŭm, | He, She, Him, Her. |
| Kenoo, | thou and I: you and I. |
| Nenĕn', | He and I: they and I. |
| Kelow', | you. |
| Nĕg'ŭmow, | They, them. |
| Sesooā', | A flame. |
| 'Ntloo'dāoo, | Smoke. |
| Tŭpkwŏn, | Ashes. |
| Booksook, | Fuel. |
| Wĭgwŏm, | A wigwam. |
| Wĕnjeegwŏm, | A house. |
| Tāpatat'-k, | A potato. |
| Wĕnjoosoon, | An apple. |
| Igŭnŭmooe, | Give it to me. |
| ĭgŭnŭmool', | I give it to thee. |
| Moo ĭgŭnŭmooloo, | I don't give it to thee. |
| Ma ĭgŭnŭmooloo. | I will not give it to thee. |
| Igŭnŭmooltĕs', | I will give it to thee. |
| Kāān', | Thank you. |
| Wĕlaalĭn, | { you do me a favor, *I am obliged.* |
| Sooleāwā', | Money. |
| Wĭsow-sooleāwā', | Gold, (*yellow money.*) |
| Wĕnjoo'sŭgĕbbun, | The turnip. |
| Eskŭdŭmŭgāwā', | { The cucumber, (*eaten raw.*) |
| Echkŏŏchk-ool, | The Pumpkin. |

| | |
|---|---|
| Peās'kŭmŭn-ŭl, | Indian corn. |
| Peāskŭmŭnŭskŏŏl, | { Corn-stalks, husks, *and* cobs. |
| Soomălke-el. | A copper. |
| Sĕnsŭl, | Cents. |

---

## L E S S O N  24.

| | |
|---|---|
| Kakŭjoomân-ŭl, | Wintergreen-berries. |
| Kakŭjoomânŏkse-el, | Wintergreen-berry plants. |
| Adooŏmkemĭn'-k, | Strawberries. |
| Adooŏmkemĭnŏk-seek, | } Strawberry plants. |
| Upkwemân-ŭi | Blue-berries. |
| Upkwemanŏkse-el, | Blue-berry bushes. |
| Usogomân'-ŭl, | Bunch-berries. |
| Usogomânŏkse-el, | Bunch-berry plants. |
| Kŭledâk', | Rasberries. |
| Kŭledow', | A Rasberry. |
| Kŭledomânŏkse-ek, | Rasberry bushes. |
| Ajeŏkchemĭn-k, | Blackberries. |
| Ajeŏkchemĭnŏkse-ek, | Blackberry bushes. |
| Mooïnomân-ul, | { Huckleberries, (*Bear berries.*) |
| Mooïnomânŏkse-el, | Huckleberry bushes. |
| Upsoolemân-ŭl, | The choke-berry. |
| Upsoolemanŏkse-el, | Choke-berry bushes. |
| Kŭlŭmooĕjemĭn'-k', | Bilberries. |
| Looemân'-ŭl, | Choke-cherries. |
| Nĭbŭmân-ŭt, | Bush-cranberries. |

| | |
|---|---|
| Nlbŭmanŏkse-el, | A Bush-cranberry tree. |
| Soon-ŭl, | Marsh-cranberries. |
| Soonŏkse-el, | Cranberry plants. |
| Nootkājemân-ŭl, | Bog-cranberries. |
| Nootkājemânŏkseel, | Bog-cranberry plants. |
| Wĭskemân'-ŭl, | Upland-cranberries, |
| Wĭskemânŏkseel, | Upland-cranberry plants. |
| Maskwāsemân-ŭl, | Wild cherries. |
| Maskwāsemanŏkse-el | The Wild cherry tree. |
| Wāgwŏnŭmĭn-k', | Black cherries. |
| Wāgwŏnŭmĭnŏkseek, | Black cherry trees. |
| Upsāmânŭl, | Roundtree berries. |
| Upsămooseel, | Roundtrees. |
| Poogoolooskwemântŭl | Elder-berries. |
| Poogoolooosk'w, | Pith-elder-wood. |
| Esnaksawaajĭk, | Clusters. |
| Poogoolooskweman-ŏkseel, | { Elders. |
| Kooŏsŭnemân ŭl, | Tea-berries. |
| Kooŏsŭuemânŏkse-el, | Tea-berry plants. |
| (Kooŏsŭn, | An old moss-covered log.) |
| Aswemânŭl, | Wine-berries. |
| Aswemânŏkseel, | Wine-berry plants. |
| Kadōmĭnk, | Swamp Raspberries. |
| Kadomĭnŏkseek, | S. R. bushes. |
| Umkooōgemĭnk, | " Bake-apples." |
| Umkooōgemĭnŏk-seek, | { " Bake-apple " plants. |
| Mĭsemĭnk, | Wild Currants: Currants. |
| Mĭsemĭnŏkseek, | Currant bushes. |
| Cowŏkchĕchkŭl, | Goose-berries. |
| Cowŏkchĕchkemoo-seel, | { Goose-berry bushes. |

| | |
|---|---|
| Kōgŭmĭn-k, | Thorn berries. |
| Kōgŭmĭnŏkseek, | Thorn trees. |
| Kastemânŭl, *and* kastŭkemânŭl, | Ground hemlock berries. |
| kastŭk, | Ground hemlock. |
| Upskŭnâk'ŭn-ŭl, | Withe-rod berries. |
| Upskŭnâkŭnemoo-seel, | Withe-rod shrubs. |
| Uchkoolchemânŭl. | Dogwood berries. |
| Uchkoolchemânŏk-seel, | Dogwood bushes. |
| Toogemanŭl, | Sheep-berries. |
| Toogemanŏkseel, | Sheep-berry bushes. |
| Chĭkchowëgŭnĕch-k', | Rose berries- |
| Chĭkchowëgtinĕch-wemooseek, | Rose bushes. |
| Malĭpkânch-ŭl, | Hazel-nuts. |
| Malĭpkânchemooseel, | Hazel-bushes. |
| Sooömân-ŭl, | Beech-nuts. |
| Sooömooseel, | Beeches. |
| Mĭmkwŏk'ŭn-ŭl, | Acorns. |
| Mĭmkwŏnmooseel, | Oaks. |
| Lĭpkŭdămoonemânŭl, | Lady's Slipper berries. |
| Lĭpkŭdămoonk', | Lady's Slippers. |
| Upkânŭl, | Nuts. |
| Upkanemooseel, | Nut-bearing trees. |
| Alogomânŭl, | Grapes. |
| Alogomânŏkseel, | Grape-vines. |
| Cowĭksaak. | Thorns, |

# LESSON 25.

## FLIES AND INSECTS,

Wechow, plur. wechâk, the fly.
Wechās-k, the house fly.
Wŏsogoweech-k, the lightning-bug.
Tĕdooĕjĭt, the Horn-bug.
Tĕdooĕjĭjĭk, (plur.) horn-bugs.
'Msĕsok, the Horse-fly.
Pĭjegŭnjĭt, the Mosqueto.
Owŏĕjĭt, the spider.
Owoĕjĭjĭk, spiders.
Kŭllumooĕch'-k, black flies. Mosquetoes
Wŏbegatajeejĭt, the sand-fly.
Uksĭpsooncheech-k, the gnat.
Tāĭpkŭmoo's-k, the water-skipper.
Saabooĕjĭt, the Dragon-fly.
Cŭmāās, the Beetle.
Lĭpsokŭnkwāowch'-ŭk, the grasshopper.
Mĭraegĕch-k, the butterfly.
Cookoogwāsees-k, the Miller.
Coolbatkĕch'-k, the Maggot.
Booktāw!t, the ladybird.
Booktāwĭjĭk, ladybirds.
Enkĕjĭt, the caterpillar.
Enkĕjĭjĭk, caterpillars.
Wĕde-ek, the worm.
Sakadeăăch-k, the dragon-fly.
Mĭsemĭnkŭnow', the locust.
Chĭgŭjeieech-k. the snail.

| | |
|---|---|
| Kelegwĕjĭt, | the pismire. |
| Amooow, | the hornet. |
| Amooāk', | Hornets. |
| Amooās'-k, | the yellow wasp. |
| Mechĭpchămooĕch, | { the Honey-bee: (the Bumble-bee.) |
| Mechĭpkei', | I store up food. |
| Edowwā', | I beg. |
| Edowŏktŭmei'. | I go round begging. |
| Edowoktŭman', | you go round begging. |
| Edowŏktŭmat', | He goes round begging. |
| Lesmaase, | { Lie down, (said to a person. |
| Lesenāān, | Lie down, (said to a dog.) |
| Pedaak, | Long. |
| Pedâtpât', | He has a long head. |
| Pedălooŏt', | He has a long tail. |
| Kĕlnŭk', | I hold him fast. |
| Kĕlătpaalŭk, | I grasp him by the head. |
| Kĕlătpĕnk', | I hold him by the head. |
| Kĕlălooaalŭk, | I grasp him by the tail. |
| Kĕlălooĕnk', | I hold him by the tail. |
| Kĕlegadaalŭk, | I grasp him by the foot. |
| Kĕlegadĕnk', | I hold him by the foot. |
| Ooseskoon, | his nose. |
| Kĕleskoonaalŭk, | I grasp his nose. |
| Kĕleskoonĕnk', | I hold him by the nose. |
| Boonăjĭm. | Let him alone. |
| Boonăjĭme', | Let me alone. |
| kĕlĭlnooaalŭk sesĭp. | I grasp a bird by the tail. |
| kĕlĭlnooĕnk' sesĭp, | I hold a bird by the tail. |

## LESSON 26.

| | |
|---|---|
| Wĕskāwenaak, | A happy land. |
| Unpōgŭn, | A Bed, |
| Mootpoon, | An animal's bed. |
| Koospĕm, | A Lake. |
| Kŭsawōk, | Iron. |
| Ooskŭnaakw, | Steel. |
| Skŭloos'k-ool, | Lead, Shot. |
| Wĕgadĕsk', | Northern Lights. |
| Wŏsĭtpaak, | A light night. |
| Nĕdoogoole, | I go a hunting. |
| Nootkāāgooei' | I hunt rabbits. |
| Nĕdooögwāăsā, | I hunt porcupines. |
| Noodogwă', | I dig them out. |
| Wĭskomāāsâ, | I creep on the moose. |
| Nĕdoomskwā, | I hunt beavers. |
| Kĕskooskwă', | I hunt bears. |
| Nebōsŭlei, | { I hunt porcupines by night. |
| Nĕdooaagwă', | I hunt seals. |
| Pemei, | I hunt birds. |
| Egwĭjaadoo, | I put it on the water. |
| Pakasaadoo, | I place it in the water. |
| Pakasaase, | { I place myself in the water. |
| Kwĕdabĕgwijaadoo, | I dip it under water. |
| Kĕdabaadoo, | I sink it in water. |
| Kwĕdabâkŭm, | I press it under the water |

| | |
|---|---|
| Kwĕdabaktĕsŭmŭk' | I dash him under water. |
| Kwĕdabaktĕsdoo, | I dash it under water. |
| Nakŭneegā', | I dip up water. |
| Nakŭnaam, | I dip it up. |
| Nĭgŭnegei, | { I dip into molasses, fat, &c. |
| Cheemā', | I paddle a canoe. |
| Pĕmeā', | I walk. |
| Pĕmeebe, | I run. |
| Elookwā, | I work. |
| Kĕloo'se, | I am good, *or* pretty. |
| Kĕloose, | I speak. |
| Etlăwĭstoo, | I talk. |
| Tĕlooā', | I say. |
| Kŭlooswŏk'ŭn, | A word. |
| Memăje, | I live. |
| Memăjooŏkŭn, | Life, |
| Tĕlsŭtŭmŭmk', | A report, a rumor. |
| Tĕlsŭtŭmei', | I hear a rumor. |
| Tĕlsŭtŭm, | It sounds so to me. |
| Kespŭnă', | I am tired. |
| Moo kespŭnow. | I am not tired. |
| Moo kespunowŭn. | You are not tired. |
| Mălāĭn, | You are lazy. |
| Moo mălāu, | I am not lazy. |
| Mălāe, | I am lazy. |
| Măloltĭjĭk, | They are lazy. |
| Moo mălolteekw, | They are not lazy. |
| Ulnook' moo mălolteekw. | } Indians are not lazy. |
| Tĕleâk' tŭ nŭt? | Is that true? |
| Meamooch' tĕleâk'. | Certainly it is true. |
| Lōk wĕledaase | I am very glad |

| | |
|---|---|
| ootŭleânŭ, | that it is true. |
| Tăleâk' ăgŭnoodŭm-âkŭn? | What is the news? |
| Mogwā' tăleanook, | There is no news. |
| Wĕledaase nĕmool. | I am glad to see you. |
| Noodŭm, | I hear it. |
| Noodŭmei', | I hear of it. |
| Ankăptĕgā', | I look. |
| Ankăptŭm, | I look at it. |
| An-kâmk', | I look at him. |
| Ankamool', | I look at thee. |
| Ankaptŭmool', | I look at thine. |
| Mĭjese', | I eat. |
| mĭjesĭn', | you eat. |
| mĭjesĭt, | he eats. |
| Nĕsăm'ookwei, | I drink. |
| nĕsăm'ookwŏn. | you drink. |
| nĕsăm'ookwŏt. | he drinks. |
| Elookwā', | I work. |
| ĕlookwĕn, | you work. |
| ĕlookwĕt', | he works. |
| Châkŭlāe, | I bustle. |
| chakŭlāĭn, | you bustle. |
| chakŭlāāk, | he bustles. |
| Sănkāwāe, | I am tranquil. |
| Sănkāwāĭn, | you are tranquil. |
| Sănkāwāāk, | he is tranquil |

### DUAL.

| | |
|---|---|
| Sănkāwāeekw, | you and I are tranquil. |
| Sănkāwāeĕk', | he and I are tranquil |
| Sănkāwāeŏk', | you *two* are tranquil |
| Sănkāwāāgĭk, | they two are tranquil |

PLURAL.

Sănkāwōlteekw, *you* and *we* are &c.
Sankāwōlteĕk', *they* and *I* are &c.
Sănkāwōlteŏk', you all are &c.
Sănkāwōltĭjĭk, they all are tranquil.

1. Sebe
2. Sebin, } To yawn : to stretch.
3. Sebĭt,

1. Mĕtpe,
2. Metpĭn, } To encamp in the open air.
3. Mĕtpĭt,

1. Coogeā',
2. Coogeĕn', } To fall and pitch the head into the water.
3. Coogeĕt,

1. Weewe,
2. Weewĭn, } To load one's self up: to put on one's load.
3. Weewĭt,

1. Ketŭnŭmei',
2. Ketŭnŭmân', } To be exhausted with labour and hardship.
3. Ketŭnŭmât',

1. Koogwaase,
2. Koogwaasĭn, } To get down on one's hands and knees to drink.
3. Koogwaasĭt,

1. Keoosā',
2. Keoosĕn', } To come upon moose or carribou in their yard.
3. Keoosĕt',

Kĕmaadĕk, A good rousmg fire.

1. Kĕmaadĕnŭmei',
2. Kĕmaadĕnŭmân', } To have a good rousing fire.
3. Kĕmaadĕnŭmât',

1. Kĕjĭp'sŭme,
2. Kejĭp'sŭmĭn, } To drink from a bucket
2. Kĕjĭp'sŭmĭt,

| | |
|---|---|
| 1. Keejŭbā, | } I have quenched my thirst, *thou* &c., *he* &c. |
| 2. Keejŭbĕn, | |
| 3. Keejŭbĕt, | |
| Maskwe, | Birch bark. |
| ŭsogom'-tāsoonĕmeek, | is of six kinds. |
| 1. Maskwe, | Birch bark. |
| 2. Bapkookāwā, | B. b. peeled in season. |
| 3. Upkconegwe, | B. b. peeled in season. |
| 4. Ulnăskwe, | B.b. peeled out of season. |
| 5. Sŭnsegwŏn, | B. b. peeled in winter. |
| 6. 'Msooĭgwe, | B. from an old dead birch. |
| Ookwuŭn, | A moose's under-lip. |
| oosoogoone, | A beast's tail. |
| wĭlneel, | A bird's tail. |
| kĕlĭlnaalŭk, | I grasp a bird by the tail. |
| kĕlĭlnĕnk', | I hold a bird by the tail. |

---

## LESSON 27.

Tan ŭmskwĕs poktŭmkeaak Kŭlooswŏkŭn
When first it begun [The] Word
āhkŭp, ak Kŭlooswŏkŭn tĕgwăooobŭnŭl Niks-
was, and [The] Word was with God,
kamul, ak Kŭlooswŏkŭn Nikskamâwĭp. Na
and [The] Word God-was. Now
Nĕgŭm tan ŭmskwĕs poktŭmkeaak, tĕgwāooŏb-
He when first it begun, was with
ŭnŭl Nĭkskamŭl. 'Msit cogooāăl wĕje-kesedăs-
God. All things by were
ĭksŭbŭnĭgŭl Nĕgŭm ootenĭnk, ak tan cogooâ
made His body, and what thing

Nĕgŭm moo kesedooksŭp, na moo kesedăsen-
He not made that not was
ooksŭp. Memăjooŏkŭn ootenĭnk āhkŭp, ak na
made. Life his body in was, and that
memăjooŏkŭn memâjooenook' oowŏsogwĕgŭ n-
life peoples' their light
ooow' na. Ak wŏsogwĕk wŏsădĕk bogŭnĭtpaak
[was] that And light shines darkness
ĭktook ak bogŭnĭtpaak moo wĕswadoogoop. Na
in and darkness not received it. Now
cheenŭmâk' wĕjĭlkemootŭnâk Nĭkskam-āwĭk-
man from was sent God within
took, tanâk tĕlooestbŭnâk San. Nĕgŭm pĕge-
who was named John. He came
sĭnkŭp oochit' ootŭlooedŭmăsoodĭn oochit' na
because of his to be a witness because of that
wŏsogwĕgŭ ; koolaman' 'msĭt wĕnĭk oowooĭkt-
light; in order to every one their irom
lamsŭtŭm-oodĭnow ootenĭnk. Nĕgŭm moo nĕg'-
believing his body in. He not that
ŭla wŏsogwĕgŭ, kadoo ĕlĕ-aboo-gwĕdoomkŭs
light, but for was sent
oochit' ootŭloowedŭmăsoodĭn oochit' na wŏsog-
because of his being a witness because of that
wĕgŭ. Na tĕt āhkŭp kĕdlāwāe-wŏsogwĕk
light. Now there was true light
tan wŏsogwadooŏch 'msĭt memăjooenŏŏ' tane
which lightens all persons who

pĕjedaalĭje oosĭtkŭmoogŭ.  Oosĭtkŭmoo'k āhkŭp
come     the world into.     In the world he was
ak  oosĭtkŭmŏŏ'  wĕje-kesedăsĭgŭp  ootenĭnkŭ, ak
and the world     by was made        his body, and
oosĭtkŭmoo  moo  kĕjeakoobŭnŭ.      Pĕgesĭnkŭp
the world    not   did know him.      He came to
tan  ĕtluhtălegĕmĭch,  an  tane  ĕtluhtălegĕmĭch
where he was owner, and whom     he owned
mogwāch'  wĕswaloogookoobŭne:  kadoo  tane
   not        did receive him :      but  those
tāsĭlĭje wĕswalŭje ĭgŭnŭmoŏch' alsoosoode Nĭks-
who received him he gave them authority God
kam  oonejŭnĭnŭ :  nŭt  nĕg'ŭla  tane  kĕdlămsŭt-
his children to be : that (is) those who     believe
ŭmoodĭlĭje oowesoonŭmkŭ.  Tanĭk  moo  wĕjuh-
his name in.          Who  not from are
skĭjenoolteekw  m âldā-wĭktook,  kŭsnâ'  maagei
    born           blood in,          nor flesh
oowooledāādâk'ŭnŭm  ĭktook,  kadoo  wĕjuhskĭje-
    its will          in,      but      from are
nooltĭjĭk  Nĭkskam-āwĭktook.
born       God        in.
     Ak Kŭlooswŏkŭ n ăwageiwasĭgŭp ak ĕtlŭgâtk-
     And  Word     became flesh and    dwelt
ŭp tan āŭmoodeek w, ak nĕmedoo'deĕgŭp ookoop-
   where we are,   and    we saw            his
medāādâkŭnŭm ;  stŭgă  Wĕgwĭsĭt  Nĭkskam
     glory            like as the Father    God

Nāooktoobĭstăjŭl    Ookwĭsŭl    ookoopmedāādâk'-
 his one only     His Son              his glory
ŭnŭm ;   wŏjooeĕch   wĕlaltĭmkāwā,  ak  kĕdlāwāoo-
            he is full of      grace     and      truth.
ŏkŭn.—John I :  1-14.

Sāsoos  ŭsĭdăboogooĕt' ak     ālăjŭl:   Tĕleâk,
 Jesus        answers    and says to him : Truly,
tĕleâk, tĕlemool,  moo wen  mĭnwuhskĭje-nooĭkw,
truly, I say to you, no one who not again is born
ma kesenŭmedookw Nĭkskamŭl ootĕlĕgāwagĭmŭ-
not   can he see       God     his kingdom.
Moo ŭkpakŭleiu 'ntŭlemoolĭn': Meamooch dĕp-
Not be surprised at my telling you: Certainly it
kadĭk  ŭkmĭnwuhskĭjenooltĭnowŭ.   Ak   stŭgă
is necessary your being born again.   And    as
Mooyeesōk  tĕle-oonagalâb'ŭnŭl  'mtāskŭmool
 Moses      so lifted up him      the serpent
bâktâkŭmĭktook,  meamooch' dĕpkadĭk  ootŭle-
the wilderness in,  certainly it is necessary  his
oonagalooksĭn Ulnoo Ookwĭsŭl , koolamân' 'msit
being lifted up  Man   his Son, in order that every
wen tan kĕdlamsŭtkŭl ootenĭnk  moo ŭksŭgawis,
one who   believes his body in, not should be lost,
kadoo ooskōs ăpchememŏjooŏk ŭn.   Mŭdŭ Nĭks-
but would have    eternal life.      For    God
kam  moo  wĕjĭlgemagoob'ŭnŭl Ookwĭsŭl oosĭt-
     not    for did send him      his Son       the

kŭmoogŭ oochĭt' ootoonmăje-ĭlsoodŭmŭn oosĭt-
world into because of his condemning       the

kumoo, kadoo wĕjĭlgĭmâb'ŭnŭl koolamân' oosĭt-
world,   but  for  he   sent him in order that the

kumoo    oochutsŭtân'   ootenink.
world   might be saved by his body.

---

## LESSON 28

### NAMES OF PLACES.

(The Indian name for the whole country, is Megumaage, MICMAC-LAND, or *Country of the Micmacs.* They divided it into seven districts, each district having its own chief, but the chief of Cape Breton, which comprised one district, was looked upon as head of the whole. As marked on the "wampum belt," C. B. is at the head. To his right stretch away three districts with their chiefs, viz., Pictou, Memramcook, and Restigouche; and the same number to the left, viz: Eskegāwaage, (from Canso to Halifax,) Shubenakadie, and Annapolis, which reaches to Yarmouth, These two arms of the country are named from two prominent points, viz., *Cape Chignecto,* and *Cape Negro*—Sĭgŭnĭkt, and Kĕs-poogwĭt. All the inhabitants of the former are designated, Sĭgŭnĭktāwâk', Sĭgŭnĭktians : and those of the later, Kĕspoogwĭtŭnâk', Kespoo-gwitians. The meaning of these two names is sufficiently plain. Kĕspoogwĭt', means : *The land's end.* Sĭgŭnĭkt is a *sock,* or *cloth for the foot,* and the reason for its application is a *Legend* too long for insertion here.

In the following list the English name is first given and printed in *small Capitals* or *Italics.* The Indian name with its signification, when known, follows. When the meaning is considered doubtful, this is printed in Italics. The list is very far from including all the Indian names.)

N. B.—I have usually given the Indian names in *the Locative Case.* The *k at the end* marks this.

---

# A.

ABEGUNBEK: Abegŭnbāāk ; 'a bending bay.'

ARCHIBALDS' MILLS, (Up. Musquedobit), Kes-okĕdĕk, 'the road runs over a hill.'

ANNAPOLIS RIVER ; Tāwōpskĭk, 'flowing out between rocks.'

AVON RIVER, Tooetŭn-ook', 'a river's mouth.'

ARGYLE ; Bapkoktĕk.

AYLESFORD BOG, Kobetek ; 'the beaver,'

ARICHAT ; Nelĭksaak', 'a split rock.'

ANTIGONISH, Nălegĭtkooneĕch; 'where branches are torn off,' viz., by the *bears gathering beechnuts.*

ABOOSHAGUN, Naboosâkŭn.

ALMEC BAY, Elmŭgwadăsĭk, 'the head is turned to one side.'

APESOOSKAM LAKE, Kesâpskŭl; 'Shining Rocks.'

ASUMEGUATAKUN, Asŭmŭtkwāāgŭn, 'head winds.'

ANDREWS BROOK, Kegŭlŭgojooïtk', 'the water tumbles and dashes in all directions.'

APPLE RIVER : Agoomâkŭn, 'Herring Fishery.'

ASHMUTOGUN ; Ukpŭdĕskâkŭn ; 'where they blockade the passage way,' viz: *where the seals go in and out,* in order to kill them. Kĕbejokoochk, 'a closing of the passage,' *is another name for Ashmutogun,*

## B.

BRAS D'OR LAKE, Petoo'bok', 'a long dish of salt water.'

BRAS D'OR ENTRANCE, Banoskĕk, 'opening out into a meadow.'

BIG POND, near the Bras d'Or, Nāookteboogooïk, 'it stands alone.'

BUCTOUCHE, Chebooktoosk, 'a small big harbour.'

BEDEQUE, C. B., Ebădĕk, 'a sultry place.'

BIRD ISLAND, Cloopske-ākăde, 'Murre-land.'

BLUE MOUNTAINS, *Yar. Co.,* Cookwĕjook, 'the spectres.'

BOOT ISLAND ; Cādebŭnegĕk'; 'clam-digging.'

BEAVER HARBOUR, Cobetāwā kwemoode 'beaver harbour.'

BROOKLYN, Queens Co. N.S., Câtcoochk, *prob. for camacoochk,* 'a hill on the opposite side.'

BRICKKILNS' Cooldanegoochk, 'the neck cord.' (*Five Islands* are supposed to form the *body* of a *moose:* Economy head is his *head.*)

BEAR RIVER ; Elsĕtkook, 'flowing along by high rocks.'

BULLS GUT, Emcokchăjĭt, 'a toad.'

BURNT CHURCH, Eskĭnwŏb'ŭdĭch, 'a lookout.'
HARRINGTON, Mĭnĭstŭgĕk.

BLOMIDON, Owbogegĕchk, 'Dogwood grove:'
*also* Mĕdogwŏtkĕk, 'bushes extending down the
bank:' *also,* Utkogŭnchechk, 'bark doubled and
sewed together.'

BRIDGEPORT ; Mĭlāsŭk ; 'plenty, abundance:
rich place.'

BELFAST, P.E.I., Mĕgwasā', 'red bank.'

BARTIBOG, Nĕbĕltook, ' *dead river,*' (or perhaps
ĕbĕltook; *'overlooked.'*)

BRULE HARBOUR, Segooāāk ; 'empty.'

BAY VERTE ; Wâkogŭmegĕk, 'lands' end.'

BEAVER HARBOUR, Wŏlŭnkâk', ' a cove.'

BATHHURST ; Wĭnpĕgĭj'ooĭk, 'a rough stream.'

BOSTON BANK ; Oonjĭktook, 'a head.'

BIG KESPABAEDAK, Kĕskabĕgeâchk', 'wide-
flowing.'

BAY CHALEUR, Mowebâktăbāāk,' biggest bay.'

BASS RIVER ; Mĭmskoolâchk': 'winding river.'

BROOKLYN, (Newport, N. S.) Nelegâkŭmĕk,
'broken snowshoes.'

BAIE DU VIN, N. B., Nĕbĕltook, *'dead river'*
*or perhaps,* ' *over-looked: neglected.'*

BROAD RIVER LAKE; QU. CO., Wobeākăde,
'resort of swans,' *'swan-land.'*

BATHURST HARBOUR ; Kĕbâmkeâk': 'stopped
by a sand bar.'

# C.

CHIMEGWE : Oosŭmoogwĭk, *'horned river.'*

CHIMEGWE RIVER ; Oosŭmoogweesk, ' *little
horned river.'*

CHEDABUCTO BAY, Sedabooktook; 'running far back.'

CAPE BRETON ; Oonămaagĭk.

CLAM HARBOUR ; Aāsŭgâdĭch, 'clam-ground,'

COUNTRY HARBOUR ; Anŭkwākăde ; 'flounder-ground.'

CANSO, Camsōk; 'opposite a high bluff.'

LITTLE CANSO, Camsogooch ; 'little camsōk.'

CARRIBOU ISLAND ; Comagŭnŭk', 'where birds are decoyed.'

CUMBERLAND, (*Fort Cumberland*) Kwĕsow-mălegĕk', 'a hard wood point.'

CAVENDISH RIVER, P.E.I. Kĭkcheboogwĕk; 'flowing along close up.'

CASCUMPEK ; Câskâmkĕk', 'a bold steep sandy shore.'

CAPE DOLPHIN, Cookŭmĭjenagwânâk: 'our grandmother.'

CAPE NEGRO ; Kĕspoogwĭtk ; 'lands' end.

CAPE ST. GEORGE, Mĕmkāch', 'a cleared field.'

CAPE SPLIT, Plekteok ; 'huge handspikes for breaking open a beaver-dam.'

The STRAIT at *Blomidon,* Pleegŭn ; 'the opening in a broken beaver-dam.'

CAPE ENRAGE ; Tĕjeegoochk, 'sail-shaped.'

CAPE MISPEC, Mĕspaak, 'over-flowed.'

CAPE TRAVERSE, Bŭslooākăde, 'sea-cow ground.'

CAPE SPRY ; Noogoomkegāwāchk', 'soft sand.'

CAPE SHUBENACADIE, Kĭtpooākăde ; 'eagle-haunt.'

CAPE NORTH, Uktŭtŭnook: 'highest mountain.'

CHESTER, Mĕnskwaak, '*I go to bring him.*'

COUNTRY HARBOUR, Moolăboogwĕk', 'deeply gullied out.'

CORNWALLIS RIVER, Chĭjĭkwtook, 'narrow river.'

CHEZZETCOOK ; Sĕsĕtcook.

CHIGNECTO, Sĭgŭnĭkt; 'a foot-cloth.'

CARRAGET HARBOUR ; Călŭgĕt.

CHRISTOPHER RIVER, Oochoo'such ; 'let the wind blow.'

CANARD RIVER, Apchechkŭmoochwākăde; resort of the black duck.

CANTICOOK, Kŭnĕtcook.

CACKMAGUN, Cookŭmeegŭn, (perhaps Cootŭmeegŭn ; '*your hatchet.*')

CHIVERIE, Wŏbooĕk, 'white water.'

CHIVERIE SPLIT, Nāeādĭch, 'heaving in sight.'

CHEGOGUN, Noojeōgŭnŭk.

CHIVERIE POINT, Nāooktooboogooedĕk', ('a tree standing by itself.')

COW BAY ; Noolŏktoochk, 'bivouacking place.'

COLE HARBOUR ; Wonpaak : 'still water.'

CRAWFORDS' FALLS ; Kĕkâkskĭtk, 'obstructed flowing.'

CRANE ISLAND, Tŭmgwŏlĭgŭnĕch'-wāākăde, 'haunt of the crane, (*heron*).'

CLYDE RIVER, Oonĭgŭnsŭk ; 'a portage.'

CHEBOGUE ; Utkŭbōk, 'a cool spring of water.'

COBEQUID, Wākobegĭtk', 'the end of the waters' flow.'

CHARLOTTETOWN, P.E.I., Booksāāk, ' a narrow entrance between steep rocks,'

# D.

*Devil's Rock,* Mŭndooŏpscoochk, 'devil's rock.'

*Digby Neck,* Oosĭtooŏkŭn, 'an ear,'

*Debert River,* (Martin's Point) Wŏsoksegĕk' ; 'seen in the distance as a signal'

*Dunk's Cove,* Oonĭgŭneenŭch, 'a portage.'

*Devil's Island,* Chĕkwchĕgwĭtk.

*Duck-Island,* Mooeownoogul, 'haunt of the sea duck.'

# E.

*Eskusone,* C. B., Eskeso'gŭnĭk.

*Eelground,* (Miramichi,) Nenădooŏkŭn, 'where eels are speared in the mud.'

*Egmont Bay;* Wegwāāk, 'turning suddenly.'

*Eeel-brook,* (Yar. Co.) Wĭpkoomāāgâkŭn; 'where poor lean fish are taken.'

*Eel River*; Okpĕgŭnchĭk, 'discoloured foam on the water.'

*Elmtree River,* Wŏbaboo-ŏkchŭk; 'white waters.'

*Ecumseekum ;* Mĕgwāsāāgŭnk ; 'a red house.'

*Economy*; Kĕnōme.

# F.

*Ford Ellis,* Mădawāāk; 'where the river branches off.'

*The Falls,* Câpskw ; 'a cascade.'

*The Grand Falls,* (above Tobique,) Chĭgŭnĭkpe, 'the roaring destroying giant.' (A terrific personage of legendary fame, whose name—*so we surmise*—was transferred to this cataract).

*French River,* Câkpĕsāgâkŭn, 'smelt-ground.'

*Five Islands,* Nankŭl mŭnegool ; 'five islands.'

*Fox Island;* Sebĕlōgwŏkŭn, ' where skins are stretched.'

*Ferguson's Bank,* Chĭgook.

*Fish Lake,* Wāāgwŏsk, 'Lake's end.'

(and Pĕskĕbāāk, is a small lake branching off from *Wagwosk*).

*Fort Lawrence,* Cwĕsomălegĕk, 'hard wood point.'

# G.

*Grand Lake,* Tŭlŭgadĭk, 'camping ground.'

*Grand River,* Amasĭboogwĕk', 'a long river.'

*General's Bridge,* Esŭnŭskĕk, 'the ground is hard and grassy.'

*Grand Manan;* Mŭnanook.

*Gaspereaux River,* (Horton) Mâgâpskegĕchk'; 'tumbling over large rocks.'

*Governor's Island;* P.E.I., Okōsĭk; 'where goods are landed.'

*Gut of Canso,* Tooegŭnŭk', 'an outlet'

*Grand Passage,* Tāāwĭtk, 'where the water flows out.'

*Glace Bay,* Wŏsekŭsegwŏn,' shining ; pellucid.'

*Grand River,* Weibooktoojeechk; 'crazy woods.'

*Grindstone Bank,* Keedâkŭnŭk, 'whetstone-rock.'

*Glenivit;* Wŏbŭmĭmskwagadĭch, '*where they gather white cranberries'*, (It may mean, ' *where they kill white porpoises.'*)

*Gross Point,* Maskwās-a-gŭmegĕk, 'a bounding in young white birch trees.'

*Garde Point,* Euchĭktoogwadĭmk, 'the place of departure, where there is risk in crossing.'

*Grand Bonaventure*; Wŏkŭmŭtkook, 'pellucid river.'

*Gaspereaux Lake,* (back of Kentville), Pasedooĕk', 'it has big whiskers;' (referring to its numerous small Islands covered with fine shrubbery).

*Gays' River,* Wĭsŭnawŏn, 'beaver castor.'

*Goose Island;* 'Mkŭdōmk, 'haunt of the black-backed gull.'

*Gibralter*; Weesĭk, 'the beaver's house.'

*Geddes Lake,* Kopskwĕdŭm-ooākăde ; 'Lamper-eel-ground.'

*Gulden Lake;* Wĕdāwaachk, 'roaring brook.'

*Green Hill,* Espakŭmegĕk'; high land.

## H.

*Halifax,* Chebooktook, 'great harbour.'

*HillsburgJi,* Elsĕtkook; 'flowing close by high rocks.'

*Horton Bluff;* Maktōmkwŭs ; 'black head.'

*Herring Point,* N. B., Wŏspooĭjĭktook : 'seal-haunt.'

*Hantsport;* Kakagwĕk', 'where meat is sliced up and dried.'

*Huckleberry Island;* Sebĭtkwĕtkŭl, flowing underneath.

*Heron Island;* Tĕsŭnŭgĕk'.

*Herring Cove, (Halifax Co.)* Moolĭpchŭgĕchk, 'a deep chasm, valley, or gorge.'

*Higgins' Brook;* Kĕskedeĕmesaak, 'a rocky ridge.'

*Horse Island;* Nĕmâkŭnatpachk', 'it has a high head.'

## I.

*Indian Town,* (near Quebec) Labooĕntŭlăbĕk'.

*Isle of Haut,* Maskoosĭtkĭk, 'an Indian potato.'

*Indian Harbour,* Utkogŭnāākăde, 'Autumn fishery.'

*Indian Road Brook,* (Shubenacadie.) Pĕbaak, '*it has a sore mouth,*' (perhaps it is, Kĕbaak, '*obstructed.*')

## J.

*Januarius* ; Nelĭksakŭjeechk, 'a small fissure.' (*probably,* simply, *Little Arichat.*)

*Jordan River;* Sesĭktāweâk', 'whimpering and whining as it goes out.'

*Jeddore;* Wĭneboogwĕchk', 'roughly-flowing.'

*Jardines Bank;* Oonĭgŭns ; 'a portage.'

*Jeddore Rock,* 'Mŭndooâpskw,' 'Rock of the Manŭtoo,' or '*great spirit*', (*now* called *the devil*)

*Jared's Point,* Cookwĕjoogwŏdĭk, 'a haunted place:' 'spectre-land.'

## K.

*Kentville,* Penooĕk ; (*prob. a man's name; Pineo ?*)

*Keskapedeak Bay;* Kĕskebeâk', 'a wide paddle.'

*Ketch Harbour* ; Nĕmāâgâkŭnŭk'; 'a [good] fishing place.'

*Kenedy's Island;* Poogesebeiĭk; 'a narrow passage, *or* channel.'

# L.

*Liverpool;* Ogomkĭgeâk', *a dry sandy place.* (*This is the exact meaning of* Pogomkĭgeâk', *and aptly enough describes the mouth of the L. river at Sandy Cove ; and the neighboring places.*)

*Lakes on the Liverpool:* No. I. Banook, see *Ponhook.* No. 2, Kĕdooskĕk. No. 3, Puhsŭgook. No. 4, Kĕjĭmkoojĭk : 'swelled parts.' No. 5, Inmŭtkaak, 'leading straight on.' No. 6, Toobeadoogook; 'lined with alders.'

*Lakeland,* (Mount Uniacke) Inskoomâdeedĭch ; 'where [hunters] respond to each other' [from adjoining lakes] by signal sounds.

*Lunenburg;* āseedĭk; 'clam-land.'

*Lenox Island;* Kĭkchesebeiĭk ; 'the passage is close in shore.'

*Lahave River;* Pĭjenooĭskâk ; 'having long joints.'

*Little Sevogul;* Elmŭnâkŭncheech; 'a beaver's hole.'

*Low Point;* Mooĭnâkŭncheechk, *'little* berrypicking place.'

*Liscomb Harbour;* Mĕgadāwĭk; 'where the big eels are taken.'

*Little River,* (Miram. N. B.) 'Mtoo'dook, 'a difficult dangerous place.'

*Long Island,* (Horton) Mĕsadĕk, 'extending far out.'

*Lawrencetown,* (Halifax Co.) Tabooesĭmkek, two parties picking berries.'

*Lafroy's Brook;* Wŏbĭmskwăgadĭch, 'where they gather white cranberries.'

*Little River,* (on the Restigouche) Kĕgŭm-oosk,' 'flowing along close up [to the upland.']

*Lake Major;* Boodĭchk, 'sitting-down place.

*Little River,* Kĕskoospāāk : 'where they catch beavers.'

*Little River,* (branch of Sheet Harbour river,) Kĕsooskowŏstoogwĕk', 'flowing among hemlock boughs.' *The other branch, is,* Ukchĭpkoodăpsk-ook, ' the largest pool.'

*Lot* 49, P.E.I., 'Ntooaagwŏkŭn, 'where seals are caught.'

# M.

*Moosaboon,* Moosăboon-ĕlagwaak ; 'a pile of hair.'

*Musquodoboit,* Mooskŭdōboogwĕk, 'flowing out square and plump.'

*Middle Musquodoboit,* Natkamkĭk, 'the river extends up hill.'

*Upper Musquodoboit;* Kesokwĕdĕk', 'the road runs over a hill.'

*An Island in the mouth of the Musquodoboit River,* is called, Amaltŭnĭk', 'variegated in appearance.'

*Memramcook;* Amlamkook ; 'variegated.'

*Middle River,* Kĕsooskowŏstoogwĕk', 'flowing through hemlock boughs.'

*Murray Harbour,* P.E.L, Eskwŏdĕk, 'the end.'

*Montagun,* Mŭntāāgŭn, 'a chunk [of pipe-stone] broken off.'

*Manadoo,* Lŭskŭch, 'a map :' 'a directory marked out.'

*Maccan River;* Māāgan, 'fishing place.'

*Madawescac;* Mădawĭskâk, 'where one river enters another.'

*Matapedia;* Mădabĕgeâk': 'roughly-flowing.'

*Mispec Cape;* Mĕspaak, 'overflowed (by the tide.')

*Meander ;* Mĭlchĕgaach,

*Merrigomish ;* Malegomĭchk, 'diversified by coves.'

*Munudie,* Mŭnoodĕk'; 'a sack,' 'a bag.'

*Malpeque,* Mâkpāāk, ' big bay.'

*Mary Joseph ;* Kŭlokwĕjook,' sculpin-ground.'

*Middle River,* C. B., Nĕmcheboogwek, 'flowing down hill in a straight course.'

*Magdalene Islands ;* Mŭnagesŭnook,

*Mudbridge,* (Wolfville) 'Mtaban, 'mud-catfishground.'

*Martin's River,* Pĭktoo'jŭk ; 'small explosions.'

*Mira, C. B.,* Soolā'kăde, *(perhaps* soonā-'kăde, *cranberry-field.)*

*Middle River;* Wŏkŭmŭtkook ; 'pellucid river,'

*Malagash Cape;* Wāgwŏstŭgwĕk', 'end of the still water.'

*Mizenette Point;* Wĕchkwŏmkeâk': 'a long sand bar extending towards us.'

*Miscou Gully;* Sebĭskadâkŭncheech, 'a straightened joint.'

*Marble Head;* Wŏkŭlopskŭsow', 'a white rock,'

*McDougal's Bank ;* Maskwagŭmegĕch, 'a white-birch grove.'

*Mistouche River;* Mĭstoogook; 'a gun-wod,' *left branch of do—*

Amkooĭk; *it touches me slightly,* (perhaps *Namkooik, 'it turns off to the leeward.'*)

*Milinchiktook;* Mĭlĭgŭnāādook, 'dressed in variegated robes.'

*Mount Scumunaak;* Eskŭmŭnaak, *'a watching place.'*

*Magwosk Point;* Mĕgwasaak, ' red rock.'

*Mill Creek,* (on River Hebert;) Booktowtāāgŭn, 'fireworks.'

*Moses River;* Noogoomkeâk': 'soft and sandy.'

*Lakes on do,* No. 1, Mâkpāāchk, 'middling sized lake.'

No. 2, Magopāāchk, 'large round.'

No. 3, Mĭlăpskegĕchk', 'abounding in rocks of all shapes and sizes.'

*Muddy Creek,* P.E.I., Mŭnĕscoochk, 'little grassy island.'

*Miramichi River,* Lŭstegoocheechk.

*Martins Point,* (Londonderry) Wŏsoksegĕk ; 'bright land-mark.'

*Margaree River;* Weeŭkŭch, 'red ochre.'

*Mouth of the Margaree,* Owchaadooch ; where they get it, [the red ochre.]

## N.

*Newfoundland;* Uktâkŭmkook', 'the mainland.'

*Negowack;* Anegāwāŏk ; 'improperly situated.'

*Napan,* 'a good place to get camp-poles.'

*Niktaux,* Nĭktaak, 'river-forks.'

*New Harbour',* Okoboogwĕk, 'foaming with discolored foam.'

*Nine Mile River;* Wŏkŭmeâk', 'pellucid river.'

*Nemtage River*, Nĕmtâkâyak'; 'it extends straight up rising ground;' (you looking *up stream*, of course, in all such cases, and there being a long reach of rapids.)

*Newel River;* Wŏsetŭmooĕk, ( *Wosesumooek,* means, '*it has bright horns.*')

*Negwac Island*, Negwĕk; 'it springs up out of the ground.'

*Newport River*, Nelegakŭmĕk, 'a broken snow-shoe.'

*New Harbour*, Ansaakw; 'a lonely rock.'

*North-West Arm;* (Halifax) Wāgwŏltĭchk; 'end of the bay.'

*Noddy Quoddy*, Noodaakwŏde; 'sealing ground.'

*Nicumteaugh;* Noogoomkeâk', 'soft sand.'

# O.

*Ooneguns River*, (on the St. John) Ooneguns-ŭk, 'a portage.'

*Oak Point*, Oochogŭm ; 'the but of a tree.'

*Oak Point*, (Cornwallis), Upkwawegŭn, 'a house covered with spruce rinds,'

*Oyster Pond;* Păjedoobaachk; 'wave-dashed:' 'buried by the rolling wave.'

*Owl's Head*, Pŭjooŏpskook; 'cormorant-rock.'

# P.

*Pesequid*, (former name of Windsor Point,) Pĕsegĭtk', 'where the tide divides and flows up in a fork:' 'a split in the rushing tide.' (*Lit.* it flows split-wise.)

*Porcupine Head*; Pookŭdăpskwŏde.

*Peticodiac;* Petkootkweâk', 'the river bends round in a bow,'

*Paspebeek,* Paspĕgeâk' ; (perhaps, *Wospegeak;* 'shining up in the distance.')

*Pabos,* Pabok, 'playful water.'

*Pirate's Cove,* Tĕsogwŏde ; 'place of flakes.'

*Petite Passage*; Tāwĭtkcheechk, 'a small out-flow.'

*Prince Edward Island,* Epāgwĭt; 'reposing on the wave :' or, *in simple prose,* 'lying on the water.'

*Port Medway;* Ulgĕdook ; 'a mushroom.'

*A Branch of do,* Abootoosok, 'honey-comb rock.'

*Lakes on the Port Medway River.* No. 1, Banook; 'opening out.' No. 2, Mălĭgeâk', 'bent in different directions.' No, 3, Munegoo-skĕk', 'grassy island.' No. 4, Nâbegwŏnchŭk, 'the ship.'

*Pictou Island,* Cŭnsŭnkook.

*Parrsborough;* Owŏkŭn, 'a crossing-over place.'

*Partridge Island;* Pŭlowĕchwā, **mŭne**goo: 'partridge island.'

*Penobscot;* Banooŏpskĕk, 'opening out among rocks.'

*Port Piswick ;* Coolpĭjooĭk, 'flowing concealed [under the earth or under rocks.']

*Pope's Harbour;* Cwemoodeech; 'a small harbour.'

*Port Hood',* Cāgwĕâmkĕk, 'on a sand bar.'

*Ponhook;* Banook, 'the river opens out into a lake.' (*A common name* for the *first lake* in a series as you go up a river.)

*Port Jolli;* Emsŭk, *perhaps Pemsuk,* 'blown along by the wind.'

*Port le' Bear;* Apsĭboogwĕchk ; 'little river.'

*Point Skimmenac;* Eskŭmŭnaak, 'look-out place.'

*Pine Grove ;* Gooöa'gŭmĭkt, 'white-pine grove.'

*Port George,* (Wilmot); Gŏŏlwagwŏpskoo'chk, 'hooded-seal-rock.'

*Prospect,* Năspaadâkŭn.

*Paradise,* Nesogwāākăde ; 'place of eel wears.'

*Portage River,* (Mirimachi) Owŏkŭn, 'a portage.'

*Pomket;* Pogŭmkĕk, 'dry sand.' *A place near do.* Pogŭmkooögĭtk, 'flowing over dry sand.'

*Pictou,* Pĭktook; 'an explosion.'

*Pictou Harbour;* Poogŭnĭkpĕchk.

*Pugwash ;* Pagwĕsk ; 'a shoal.'

*Point Prim;* Wejowĭtk, 'the current flows close in.'

*Pandora Point;* Mĕmkāāk kwĕsawă': 'cleared-field point.'

*Point Miskwe;* Oonĭskwŏmkook; 'the end of a sand bar.'

*Pokeshaw ;* Pooksaak, 'a long narrow stone.'

*Portugese Cove;* Wŏlnŭmkeajechk; 'a small sandy cove.'

*Porter's Lake,* Amâkŭncheech ; *perhaps Pemakuncheech;* 'where they shoot birds on the wing.'

*Petpiswick;* Coolpĭj'ooĭk; 'the river flows along hidden under the ground or rocks.'

*Pumpkin Island;* Sŭmskwĕs.

*Pennant Point;* Skabânk'; 'where they eat raw [food].'

*Pubnico:* Pogomkook, 'dry sand.'

*Petite River,* (Hants Co.) Upskâmkook; 'a sand gully.'

*Pipe Rock,* (Miramichi) Tŭmâkŭnâpskw; 'pipe rock.'

*Pereaux;* Wŏjeechk; 'a white signal seen from afar.'

*Pokemouche Gully,* Pokŭmooch'-petooāāk; 'salt water extending inland.'

*Port Mulgrave;* Wolŭmkwā-kagŭnŭchk: 'lobster-ground.'

# Q.

*Quebec;* Kĕbĕk; 'A Strait.' 'An obstruction.' 'Narrows.'

*Quaco ;* Goolwagagĕk; 'haunt of the hooded seal.'

# S.

*Salmon River;* Anĕsaak; a solitary rock.

*St. Peter's Island;* P.E.I., Bâslooăăkâde; 'sea-cow-haunt.'

*St. Peter's;* P.E.I., Boogoosŭmkĕk; '*I give him half the food.*'

*Salmon River,* (Yar. Co.) Boonămookwŏde, 'tomcod-ground.'

*Spry Harbour;* Sebĭmkooaak; 'a bog extending across.'

*Sagunay River;* 'Ktădoosōk; 'flowing between two high steep cliffs.'

*St. Paul's Island;* Kuhtŭmŭnegoo ; 'a round island,'

*Stewiacke;* Sesĭktāweâk'; 'whimpering and whining as it goes out'

*St. Lawrence;* Mĭjeōgŭn.

*St. John, N.B.;* Mĕnagwĕs; 'where they collect the dead seals.'

*St. John River;* Oolastook; 'beautiful river.'

*St. Mary's* Naboosâkŭnŭk.

*St. Mary's River Forks,* (Pictou Co,) Nĭmnogŭn; a 'black birch tree.'

*St. Mary's Bay* head of, (Digby); Wâgweiĭk ; 'the end.'

*Sable River;* Neseâmk; 'flowing down over sand.' *Also* Pĭjeboogwĕk'; 'long river.'

*Seal Island,* (in the Bras d'Or); 'Ntooagwŏkŭncheech; 'little sealing place.'

*Sand Island,* (Miramichi); Pĕmâmkeâk'; 'a stretch of sand.'

*Smoky Head,* C.B., Sâkpeedĭch.

*Shelburne,* Sogŭmkeegŭn.

*Ship Harbour;* Tĕdŭmŭneboogwĕk; 'blunt river.'

*Sydney River;* Ulsebookt.

*Shoal Bay;* Wŏspĕgeâk': 'the water shines up in the distance.'

*Sheet Harbour;* Weijooĭk: 'flowing wildly.'

*St. Simons Inlet;* Wĭnâmkeâk'; 'a rough sandy bank.'

*Shippegan Gully;* Umkoomabāāk; 'icy bay.'

*St. Annes,* C.B., 'Mchāgadĭchk.

*Skippegan;* Sepagŭncheech; 'a duck-road:'
i.e., *a small passage through which the ducks fly
from one place to another. An island in Shippegan
River;* Booksakadĕk; 'a live coal.' *Also,* 'a narrow passage between rocks.'

*Still-water Bank,* N.B., Pĕtăwagŭmegĕk'; 'a
charred grove.'

*Slate Mountain;* Keneskwŏtpât'; 'he has a
peaked head.' *A brook near the above,* is, Egogĕk,
'next to the woods.'

*Spencer's Island;* Wochuk ; 'a small kettle.'

*Sambro Cape;* Mĕseebâkŭnŭk, 'great tobacco-
smoking place.'

*Salmon River;* (Eastern Shore, N.S.,) Boonămookwŏde, 'tomcod-ground *Lakes on the
above,* No. I. Usoogomŭsoogwĕdâmk: 'wading-
across place;' 'a ford.'   No. 2. Mĭlpāāchk, 'having many coves.'   No. 3. Utkoskwāāchk; ' the
twin-girls.'.   No. 4. Cloocheowpāāchk, 'cross-
lake.'   No. 5. Nĕmchenokpāāchk, 'cross-wise-
lying lake.'   No. 6, Noogoomkŭbāāk, 'place of
fine white sand.'   No. 7. 'Mtăbĕswāākăde,
'where mud-cat-fish abound.'

*Scraggy Lake,* Mĭsegŭmĭsk, 'scraggy & rough.'

*Starr's Point,* (Cornwallis), Nĕsoo'gwĭtk; 'it
lies on the water between [two other points].'

*Salmon River;* Pŭlămooā' seboo; 'salmon-river.'

*Saunders' Harbour;* Kĭkchesebeiĭk; 'a channel
*or* passage close in by the shore.'

*Smith's Cove;* Sĕgegŭneegŭnk; 'a canvass tent.'

*Sheshen;* Pogopskĕk; 'a dry rock.'

*Shediac,* Esĕdeiĭk, 'running far back.'

*Sand River,* (Cum. Co.) Agoomâkŭnŭk, 'where
they catch herring.'

*Shubenacadie;*    Sĕgŭbŭnāākăde;    'where
ground-nuts abound.'    'Indian-potato field.'

# T.

*Three Fathom Harbour;* Asŭgwĭtk'; *'joined
to another:* as if *Ansudek.*

*Tusket;* Aglaseāwā'kăde, 'An English settle-
ment.'

*Toney River;* Booktāwāāgĕn; *this word has
two significations, viz:* 'you lie on the side next
the fire;' *and,* 'you go for fire.'

*Table Island;* Cheegooncoochk, *'a knee.'*

*Thorn Point,* (Shediac); Cowĭksomoosegĕk;
'a grove of thorn-trees.'

*Tignish;* 'Mtagŭnĕchk', 'a paddle.'

*Three Rivers,* P.E.I., Sāāmkw.

*Tracadie;* Tŭlakădĭk, 'camping ground.'

*Little Tracadie,* Tŭlakadeech, 'little camping-
ground.'

*Tatamagouche,* Takŭmegoochk, 'extending
across.'

*Taboosintac;* Taboosĭmkĭk, 'a pair of them.'

*Tar Bay;* Upkooāākăde, 'tar *or* turpentine
region.'

*Tracy's Brook,* Egogwāsees; 'the edge of the
woods.'

*Tracadigash;* Tŭlŭgadegāchk, 'little camping-
ground.'

*Tangier;* Wŏspĕgeâk', 'the water shines up
in the distance.'

*Tangier Lakes,* No. 1. Wĭskŭsok'; 'a spruce
bud.' No. 2. *Brien's Lake,* Mĭlpagĕch: 'variega-

ted.' No. 3. Nĕnāsakŭmĕk; 'spreading out snow-shoes'. No. 4. Pĕdāwĭkpāāk; 'the flowing is obstructed in the midst of a barren.'

*Tangier River;* Nĭktooŏkpaak; 'flowing on fork-wise.'

*Taylor's Head;* Sĕgŭnagĭgŭnŭk; 'a spread sail.'

## U.

*Upsatquitch, N.B.,* Apsĕtkwĕchk; 'a small river.'

*Umkwe River;* Amkooĭk. *Prob.* 'Mkooögwĭk *'boggy.'*

## W.

*White Head;* Camsogoochech.

*Wallace;* Emsĭk, *or* Pĕmsĭk.

*White Islands;* Pŭgŭmĕjooāākâde, 'land-lizard-place;' 'abounding in land-lizards.'

*Wine Harbour,* Pŭlamkeegŭnŭchk, 'an outlet cut through the sand.'

*Windsor,* Sĕtŭn-ook; *perhaps* for *Upsetun,* 'the channel of a river.'

*Whycogumagh;* Wākogumaak', 'end of the bay.'

*Winchelsea Harbour;* Noodakwŏde; 'seal-haunt.'

*West Brook,* (running into *Kespapedeak Bay*) Tŭlabadancheech.

*Wolf River ;* Boktŭsŭmooā' seboo; 'wolf-river.

*Wolf's Island;* Pĕdawoongĕk, 'covered with fog and smoke.' (It may also mean, '*a burnt-over place,*' *Pedawogunaak.*)

*West Point;* Wŏlnâmkeâk', 'a sandy cove.'

*White Waters,* (Lower Pereaux), Wŏjeechk, 'a signal, (*a water-fall*), showing *white* in the distance.'

*White Waters,* (Chiverie); Wobooĕk, 'the water appears white.'

*West Bay, C.B. ;* Wŏlnămkeâk', 'sandy cove.'

*West River Lake;* Bŭnāākăde, 'region of darkness.'

*White Point;* Anagwāākăde; 'flounder-ground.'

# Y.

*Yarmouth River;* Mălĭgeâk'; 'winding and turning every which way.'

―――――

### THE NAMES OF THE MONTHS.

*January ;*  Boonămooe-goos';

Frost-Fish Month.

*February;*  Abŭgŭnăjĭt,

The snow-blinder.

*March;*  'Segow-goos',

Spring-month.

*April;*  Pŭnâdŭmooe-goos'.

Egg-laying month.

*May;*  Agese-goos'.

Month of young seals.

*June;*  Nĭbŭne-goos'.

Summer-month.

*Also,*  Sagĭpkegoos'.

Leaf-opening month.

*July;*   Upskooe-goos'.

> Month when the sea-fowl shed their feathers.

*August;*   Kesagāwe-goos'.

> Month when the young birds are full-fledged.

*September;*   Majowtoogwe-goos'.

> The 'running' month.'Moose-calling month.

*October;*   Wegāwegoos'.

> Fat month; (when *tame animals* are fat.)

*November;*   Skŏŏls.

*December;*   Ukchegoos'.

> The chief month, *(when christmas comes.)*

MATTHEW, Chapter 15 : 21-39.

Tokoo Sāsoos wějĭpkotŭmkaasĭt nadāālŭ, ak
Then   Jesus   from goes away   there,   and

āleějŭl Teil ak Seidun ootababĭmooŏkŭ. Ak
goes to Tyre and Sidon   their bounds.   And

ědŭ ābĭt Cānŭnkāweeskw wějeějŭl něg'ŭla ma-
lo! a woman   a Canaanitess   comes from   these

kŭmegŭl' ak ělkomĭktooājŭl, āāt: āooledāālŭme,
lands   and   calls to   him,   says : have mercy upon me,

'Nsakěmam, Dabĭd Ookwĭsul; 'ntoos lōk kěsuh-
O my Lord,   David   his son ; my daughter very much

che-oonmăjāāk mŭndoo ĭktook.   Cadoo Sāsoos
from tormented [is]   a devil   into.   But   Jesus

moo ŭseděmagool nāooktā' kŭlooswŏkŭn.   To-
not   answers her   one   word.   Then

koo kěgenoodŭmooŏje pějedalĭje tan āhkŭ, ak
those whom he is teaching   come   where he is and

ĕdămadĭjŭl, tĕlooĕjĭk : Jĭgulgĭm' ābĭt, mŭdŭ ĕtle-
beseech him,     they say : Send her away the woman, because

sāskwĕt       koodĕnâkŭ.   Cadoo  Sāsoos  ŭse-
continually she screams behind us.   But     Jesus    an-

dăboogooĕt', āāt:  Pasŭk  ĕlkemĭmk  ĕtlĭksŭgaa-
swers,       says:  Only   I am sent   there where are

dĭch  chechkĕlooāoochŭk  Islāāl  week  tŭlāāk.
lost       sheep           Israel his house belonging to.

Tokoo  ābĭt  pĕgesĭnk'  ak  ogŭlŭmkwĕdĕsĭnkŭl
Then the woman    comes   and    falls down to him

ooskalook  Sāsoosŭl,  ālăjŭl;  'Nsak'ŭmam,  abo-
before       Jesus,    says to him:  0 my Lord,     help

gŭnŭmooe !  Cadoo  Sāsoos  ŭsedăboogooĕt',  āāt:
me!     But   Jesus      answers,       says:

Moo  kĕlool'tŭnook'  sooadooŏn'  mĭjooajechk
No      good not       to take it         children

weloŏŏl'  ak  ĭgŭnŭmooŏn'  ŭlŭmoojŭgŭ.  Cadoo
their food   and   to give it to       dogs.        But

ābĭt  tĕlooĕt:  Tĕleâk',  'Nsak'ŭmam,  mŭdŭ
the woman  says :   It is true,    My Lord,     because

ŭlŭmoo'jŭk  wĕje-mĭjesooltĭjĭk  puĭbŭnĕgool  tanŭl
dogs        from        eat          crumbs       which

wĕjenese-pŭnĕgweagŭl  alsoomkweedĭje  oobăta-
from down fall    in fragments    their master    his

loodĭmooow'.  Tokoo  Sāsoos  ŭsedăboogooĕt',
table.       Then    Jesus        answers,

ālăjul:  ābĭt!  mĕskeek  ŭkŭdlămsŭtooŏk'ŭnŭm !
says to her : O woman !  great [is]         your faith !

Tŭlāāch  ŭktenĭn  tan  tĕlĭmsoonedāādŭmŭnŭ!
Let it be to  thy body   as      so you desire it.

Na ba  tĭlesĭp'  ootoosŭl  kesĭnsalooksĭlĭjŭl.
Now then at that time her daughter has been cured,

Tokoo tĭlesĭp' Sāsoos wĕjĭpkotŭmkaasĭt nadāālŭ,
Then  at that time  Jesus  from  departs  there,

ak wĕjooatĕskŭk ŭkchĭgŭm Gălelĕtkŭ ak ĕlitko-
and  comes near to  the sea  in Galilee  and  goes

jooimtŭmaat kŭmdŭn ĭktook, ak nadāāl ĕbaasĭt.
up  a mountain  into,  and  there  sits down.

Ak mowe-poogwĕlkĭk memăjooenoo'k pĕjedaajĭk
And  together many  people  come

āhkŭ ak wĭjĭtkwāooadĭje tane askasooltĭlĭje ak
where he is and  and have with them  those who are lame  and

nĕgăbegoltĭlĭje, ak tane moo nĕdowoodĭlĭgwe
blind,  and those who  not  speak,

ak tane nĕblĕptĭnadĭlĭje ak tane nĕblĕsegadadĭlĭje
and those who have but one hand  and those who have but one foot

ak poogwĕlnĭje ŭktŭge, ak egaladĭje Sāsoosŭl
and  many  others,  and put them down Jesus

ookwŏtkŭ; ak tĕlĭnsaalăje chĕl mowe-poog-
his feet at;  and  he so heals them  that  together

wĕlnĭje pakŭleiooltĭlĭje tan tĭlesĭp' nĕmeaadĭch
many  are astonished'  then  when  they see

tane moo nĕdowoodĭlĭgwe ookŭloosooltĭlĭnŭ,
those who not  speak  their speaking

ak tane nĕblĕptĭnadĭlĭje, ak tane nĕblĕse-
and those who have but one hand,  and  those who have but

gadadĭlĭje oonŭsoltĭlĭnŭ, ak tane askasooltĭlĭje
one foot  their being cured, and those who  are lame

oopŭmedalinŭ; ak kĕpmedāālŭmadĭjŭl Islāālŭl
their walking;  and  they honour him  Israel

oo-Nĭkskamŭl. Tokoo Sāsoos wegoomăje
his God.  Then  Jesus  calls them

kĕgenoodŭmooŏje ak ālăje: Aooledālŭmkĭk
whom he is teaching  and says to them :  I pity them

107

mowe-poogwĕlkĭk memăjooenoo'k, mŭdŭ ăpch-
together many people, because always

ĭtkwāooĭjĭk nāsoogoonaak ak mogwâ' wĕsko-
they are with me three days and nights and not have

dŭmeedĭkw tan kogooâ' mălkodŭmŭgŭ: ak
they what thing to be eaten; and

mogwā' wĕledāādŭmoo 'njĭgŭlgĭmân' soonā-
not I am willing for my sending them away

wĭmkāwā' ĭktook koolaman' mŏo oonowtāsa-
fasting in so that not their giving

dĭnow' owhtĭgŭ. Ak kĕgenoodŭmooŏje
out in the road. And those whom he is teaching

tĕlĭmche: Tame tĕt bâktâkŭmĭktook oochim-
teïl him: Where there the wilderness in could we

sŭnŭmoogoop ootule-tĕbeân pĭbŭnŏkŭn ŭk-
obtain its being enough bread [for] our

tŭlesŭmanĕnoo tĕle-poogwĕlkĭk memăjooenoo'k ?
so feeding them so many people?

Tokoo Sāsoos ālăje: Tasĭbŭnaagŭl kĕkoonŭm-
Then Jesus says to them : How many loaves of bread have

ogŭl ? Tĕlemaadĭjŭl: Elooĭgŭnŭk-tāsĭbŭnaagŭl,
you ? They tell him : Seven so many loaves of bread

ak tĕgĕlādĭjĭk ăpchâjooltĭjĭk nŭmāchŭgŭ. Tokoo
and a few small fishes. Then

tĕlkĭmaje mowepoogwĕlnĭje memăjooenoo'.
he commands them together many people

ootŭlesŭmedaalin makŭroegĕgŭ. Tokoo wĕswa-
their lying down on the ground. Then he takes

dogŭl nĕg'ŭla ĕlooĭgŭnŭk-tāsĭbŭnaagŭl
them these seven loaves of bread

pibŭnŏkŭnŭl ak nŭmājeŭ, ak mooewĕt' ak
loaves of bread and the fishes, and he gives thanks and

sĕgwĭskĭbŭnĕgadogŭl ak ĭgŭnŭmooŏjul kegenoo-
he breaks up the bread and gives them to those whom

dŭmooŏj'eŭ, ak kĕgenoodŭmooŏje ĭgŭnŭmooadĭje
he is teaching, and those whom he is teaching give them to them

mowe-poogwĕlnĭje memajooenoo'. Ak 'msĭt
together many the people. And all

mĭjesooltĭjĭk ak kesădălooltĭjĭk; ak wĕjĭmkŭnŭm-
eat and are satisfied; and they gather them

eedĭjŭl puĭbŭnĕgool tanŭl ĕskweâgŭl ĕlooĭgŭnŭk-
up the broken pieces of bread which remain seven

tâsŭgŭl pootăleăwāāl wĕjuh-chooeagŭl. Ak
so many baskets filled by them. And

tanĭk ĕtlădălooltĭjĭk ĕdŏŏk nāoo betooĭmtŭl-
those who eat their meal about [are] four thousand

nâkŭnĭjĭk cheenŭmoo'k ak skŭmtook ābĭjĭk
men and besides them also women

ak mĭjooajechkŭ. Tokoo Sāsoos ĕjĭgŭlgĭmăje
and children. Then Jesus sends them away

mowe-poogwĕlnĭje memăjooenoo'ŭ, tokoo tĕbaasĭt
together many people, then he gets in

wĕnjoolkoodook, ak okwaajŭl makŭmegŭl' Măg-
a vessel into, and lands at the lands Magdala

dŭlâk' tŭlāālŭ.
belonging to.

ERRATA.
Preface, 1st Paragraph *add,* except in a few pages.
Page 72, last 2 lines, for ' tail' read *Hongue.'*
" 81, for 'Shubenakadie' read ' *Skubenacadie.'*
" 82, for 'Musquedobit' read '*Musquodoboit'*

Oola' Weegădĭgŭn wĕje-le-dâkŭn-weegăsĭk Megŭmageā'
Ledâkŭnwee-kŭgĕmkāwā' Mowweōm ĭktŏŏk.

www.ingramcontent.com/pod-product-compliance
Lightning Source LLC
LaVergne TN
LVHW091200080426
835509LV00006B/760